ons that wake you up at night."

evy, author of *The Last Rebbe of Bialystok*

ing, integrating, and soothing gift! In *Epiphanies,*
helped me to locate myself as a member of a post-
community. She applies her penetrating and
-rays to some of the most important human
e. She's given me the wherewithal to answer why
c and spiritual pursuits have never seemed dis-
uestions have always been my favorite form of

Ham, M.A., cofounder of the
en's Therapy Center

mportant book. Ann Jauregui evinces her lifelong
ent with the question of the continuity and coher-
rse. As a young child contemplating the night sky,
pist listening deeply to her clients' search for mean-
tmodern thinker integrating the new paradoxes of
e and fluid uncertainty, she teaches us about whole-
prose filled with compelling personal narratives, she
integration of the cognitive, emotional, and spiritual
a conscious human being as we turn into the third

n Zucker, Ph.D., psychotherapist and cofounder of
ell House, a center for psychotherapy and training

MORE

"We are taken to the
bears a remarkable r
moments when the i
the new. With bravur
'tales of psychothera|
again as if the only bo
more than speed bum

—David Ep
Narrative M
Freeman ar
Problems: Na

"What an illuminat
Ann Jauregui has
modern scientific
synthesizing mind
concerns there ar
psychotherapeuti
parate and why q
dialogue."

—Nina
Wom

"Until now Annie Dillar
right-brained person I l
to bring my spirituality
servative path. I think Si

—Joan Herri
with Virginia
Association o

"*Epiphanies* is an i
fascination/torn
ence of the univ
as a psychothera
ing, and as a pos
mutual influenc
ness. In supple |
offers us a rare
aspects of being
millennium."

—Elle
Rus

"In these stories, personal
astonishing reminder of th
is a powerful collection of
by a wise and loving psych

—Jane Loebel,
Center and past
Therapists of N

EPIPHANIES

A Psychotherapist's Tales of
Spontaneous Emotional Healing

For Greg,
With my gratitude and my love,
Ann

ANN JAUREGUI, PH.D.

PRIMA PUBLISHING

Published by Prima Publishing, Roseville, California. Member of the Crown Publishing Group, a division of Random House, Inc., New York.

PRIMA PUBLISHING and colophon are trademarks of Random House, Inc., registered with the United States Patent and Trademark Office.

Library of Congress Cataloging-in-Publication Data
Jauregui, Ann.
    Epiphanies : a psychotherapist's tales of spontaneous emotional healing / Ann Jauregui
      p.   cm.
    Includes bibliographical references and index.
    ISBN 0-7615-6376-8
    1. Psychotherapy—Case studies. I. Jauregui, Ann. II. Title.
RC465 .J38 2002
616.89'14—dc21   2002035456

03 04 05 06 07 08 QQ 10 9 8 7 6 5 4 3 2 1
Printed in the United States of America

First Edition

Visit us online at www.primapublishing.com

For John

CONTENTS

Acknowledgments · ix
Preface · xi

Introduction · 1

1. Silver Bay and the Question of *I* · 11

2. Quantum Physics on the Car Radio · 25

3. Will the Real Reality Please Stand Up? · 39

4. Isaac Newton's Nervous Breakdown · 59

5. Mind Science · 77

6. Postmodern Psychotherapy:
   The Feet in the Foreground · 99

7. But Can You See It? · 123

8. If You Can't Meditate, Travel · 137

9. Help Already on the Way · 159

10. Homecoming · 175

Notes and Suggested Readings · 187
Bibliography · 197
Index · 205
About the Author · 210

ACKNOWLEDGMENTS

ONE EVENING, camped with good friends on the Salmon River, I was watching the purple river as it flowed along, lapping at our little flotilla of rafts and kayaks pulled up haphazardly on the beach. Lee was sitting near me, watching too.

"Lee?"

"Mm?" he answered through the dusk, probably reviewing some of the more challenging rapids of the day.

"What's the name of that yellow garden flower that starts with 'w'?"

"Coreopsis," he said.

"Coreopsis. Thank you."

"Don't mention it."

And so thanks to Lee Ballance and to all these mind-sharing friends:

To my writers' group—Mary Hidalgo, Annie Kane, Liz Raymer, Robyn Raymer, Roussel Sargent, Christy Shepherd—

for enduring the repetitions on Thursdays and keeping the faith. To Monza Naff, our fearless leader, for holding up her catcher's mitt and singing out, "Put it right in here," and for directing me to Caroline.

To Caroline Pincus, book midwife, for her enthusiasm and for directing me to Tom.

To Tom Grady, as warm and erudite a literary agent as there can be, for his companionship, guidance, and for finding Alice.

To Alice Feinstein, my editor at Prima Publishing, for her strong commitment and light touch, and to Libby Larson, my project editor, for making this such an excellent and happy adventure.

To family and friends, privately thanked, for kindly reading along, and then reading again, keeping me company in the margins. To Greg Hofmann, for urging me not to try to impersonate a science writer. To Jane Gray, Susan Hesse, Neil Levy, David Schwartz, Jack Shoemaker, in on it from the beginning, Kendra and Huston Smith, Davis Taylor, Richard Trumbull, Barbara Waters.

Thanks to Martha Cochrane, flowmeister, word dancer.

Thanks to John Jauregui, for helping me in every way a person can help, and to our children and grandchildren, deliciously wise.

ESPECIALLY, THANK YOU to all my clients for showing the way, and to those who have generously agreed to share their stories here.

PREFACE

It was the time for sitting on porches beside the road.

It was the time to hear things and talk.

ZORA NEALE HURSTON,

THEIR EYES WERE WATCHING GOD

CONTEMPORARY PSYCHOTHERAPY, like all good conversations, is up against something: The universe is a whole lot bigger than we thought. And it is getting bigger by the nanosecond. The stuff of creation is still spraying out into unimaginable depths of space from the explosion of a "grain" of matter that was, for all purposes, infinitely small and infinitely dense. The source of this grain? Nobody knows.

The Hubble Space Telescope, when pointed at one of the emptiest parts of the sky, is finding galaxies (which include, no doubt, plenty of places congenial to life) as far as its eye can see. Perhaps, cosmologists are saying, there are fifty billion of them. There is beginning to be talk of many dimensions of the universe, of many universes. With the Hubble reined back in and trained on the Milky Way's own Eagle Nebula, nursery to many young stars, one can witness a star birth. Breathtaking. Incomprehensible. A person is reduced to walking around in small circles, muttering, "I have to rethink infinity."

Meanwhile an inverse sort of hugeness, the microscopic cosmos of subatomic space, is being explored by advanced electron microscopy. Zooming down into the seemingly solid objects of our seemingly familiar world, physicists find another vast space sprinkled with occasional atoms made of constantly moving "particles" that turn out not to be particles at all. At the farthest reaches of the electron microscope eye, there seems to be nothing to see but a tendency for a "piece" of matter to show up. A wavering. Nothing more definite than a wavering.

There is no escaping it. We are living in a moment of human history in which investigators of all stripes are asking the oldest of questions against a backdrop of the newest of findings. In all this immensity—in all this mystery—what is reality and what is our place in it?

Most people don't come for psychotherapy because they are queasy about their place in an exploding universe. Not exactly. Most people come because they are experiencing some kind of misalignment in their lives. A client reports that she has written in her journal, "A good day is when the truth isn't a threat." Psychotherapy assumes that pain signals the place to go in. But with what assumptions, what maps?

In the seventeenth century, René Descartes and the other great figures of the Scientific Revolution didn't know about ephemeral matter, curved space, liquid time. They thought there was something finished, something fixed about the universe that would be comprehensible when approached scientifically, which meant objectively. For the next three hundred years, Cartesian thinking infused everything, including theories of psychotherapy that said a person's life, like the universe itself, was supposed to be fixed and comprehensible.

Now we are living in times that are being called postmodern, times in which everything is in flux. As we turn into the new millennium, much of what is being observed in the natural world defies the so-called commonsense formulations of classical science. And postmodern scientists are saying that as crazy as it looks now, the universe is going to look a lot crazier before we are through.

Spinning, we are thrown back onto ourselves, onto what Steven Jay Gould called "the irreducible importance of local detail." We are back in the center of the universe again, called upon to sustain the pluralism, and the commotion, of personal truth.

Suddenly this hapless moment shimmers with promise. From somewhere in the middle of an immense creation, we begin to reclaim our sight, hearing, smell, taste, and touch. Our dreams. Our hunches. Our curious moments of knowing someone far away is thinking of us. We begin to reclaim all this not (necessarily) out of hedonism, but because we begin to suspect that personal knowing is all the knowing we are going to get for a good long while.

The psychotherapeutic conversation, following this evolution in human thinking, makes a turn. Instead of worrying about making a person right, as if there were a right, we attend to our personal stories.

A client who has suffered a stroke has been talking about her life when she pauses. Hesitantly she says, "I just discovered something. You know the before-stroke and after-stroke 'me'? *I* . . . am in both. Untouched."

Psychotherapy is poised at the waist of the hourglass, between all of what we see outside ourselves and all of what we see inside. In the moment of quiet, the healing realization comes. It is all personal, and it is all ours.

"Where is this coming from?" my client asks—looking out, looking in—and surprised, she smiles a wonderful smile.

And so this book must be personal—not a memoir in the sense of self-portrait (although the rush to share memoirs at this moment in our development suggests a recognition that personal truth anchors us, even as the universe sprays out into trackless space) but personal in response to the new-old recognition that I and what I am looking at are the same. I and what I am looking *for* are the same.

It begins for me at Silver Bay.

INTRODUCTION

And it came to me all in a feeling how everything fitted together,
the place and ourselves and the animals and the tools, and how
the sky held us.

WENDELL BERRY,
A World Lost

WHEN I WAS a young girl—long before I ever imagined becoming a psychotherapist or even knew what psychotherapy was—something odd and wonderful would sometimes happen to me out on the raft on Silver Bay, something I never told anybody about.

Silver Bay was our summer place in the Upper Peninsula of Michigan. The raft floated on four old 55-gallon metal drums and rode high in the water, except for a plank right at water level that made it easy for a swimmer to slip in and out. I would row the boat out to the raft, tie up, and spread out in the sun with my book, glad to be by myself for a while. The raft would roll gently in the midsummer breeze of Michigan's north woods. After a little while, I would put down my book and just listen to the water slappity-slapping against the metal drums and that low board, and to the boat nuzzling and bumping up against the raft, and to the soft groan of the boat's rope. I would breathe the smells that rose up from the weathered boards, from sun-warmed skin, from the woods along the near shore, fragrances marbling the air. I would lie there and wonder about things and watch myself wondering. Sometimes I would notice that a stretch of time had gone by, and I hadn't wondered about anything at all.

Then, occasionally and unpredictably, I would feel myself come undone. In the warmth of the sun, in the sparkle of the water and clear northern light, I would suddenly bloom up out of myself, past my skin, my thoughts, my sense of place, into an airy and ecstatic hugeness.

I'm out! were the words that came to me. *And everything is alive!* The trees were alive, of course, and the fish in the bay, and the Indian paintbrush on the far shore. Everything was beating to one great heart. But the round pebbles on the beach were beating too, and the galaxies, the interior spaces of all things, the human-made-ness of human-made things. It was so clear: *Everything is life!*

And as for me? I found that I could put questions to the experience. Was there anything in particular about me in this pulsing landscape? What was my part?

I want to know, were the words that came. They came in a whisper. *Show me.* And it seemed to me that wanting to know, exactly that, was my part in this great amplitude of life—that creation delights in the recognition of itself.

After a short while or a long while, I would come back into my more familiar self. I would sort of dust myself off, gather up my towel and book, climb back into the boat, and row myself home to the cabin where my family was up to whatever they were up to, in and out, screen doors smacking.

. . .

EPIPHANY IS A big word, a thunderclap of a word. It conjures up the landscapes of mystics and saints, of Moses at the burning bush, and the Buddha under the bodhi tree.

In uppercase, "Epiphany" grew out of the Christian tradition of the late Middle Ages. In this capitalized form it refers to the festival called Twelfth Night, which celebrates the night the Magi, following a star hanging low in the winter sky, came upon the baby Jesus in a manger.

In lowercase, the word "epiphany" is much older. It first appears in the work of Herodotus, Greek historian of the fifth century B.C.E., and means "the coming to light" or "appearing of gods." Seals depicting revelations have been found on the island of Crete that are older still. The Greeks, it would seem, have been having epiphanies for a very long time and, I suspect, Neolithic folks before them.

In present day, "epiphany" refers to a sudden recognition or insight into the essential meaning of something. But my favorite part of the definition tells us that the revelation is usually brought on by some simple, homely, or commonplace experience. Something big is occasioned by something little, something easily missed. And it unfolds from there—sometimes as a flash, sometimes in exquisite slow motion—out of conventional time and space and language.

"Look at this!" you whisper as you see something about the universe that you've never seen before. "And look at *this,*" you whisper too, seeing yourself seeing it. The universe is bigger than it was a minute ago, and so are you.

But back in the cabin overlooking Silver Bay, I didn't talk about my experiences on the raft. Not talking about them seems as important to me now as the experiences themselves, and I have thought long and hard about why I didn't. Why? It was not because my family would have been uninterested or worried that I had gone round the bend. My mother was a loving person and had a strong metaphysical turn of mind. She would have listened carefully to me, and she might have told me stories of her own. My father knew from his athletic prowess the thrill of being in the "zone," moving through time and space as if he were being moved by something bigger. We told stories about these things.

"Why didn't I?" I asked my brother recently, wondering out loud about why I didn't tell anybody back then. "It seems to me now that those experiences were so big and yet so . . . what?"

"Abstract," he suggested. "The other night I heard a jazz musician try to explain how hard it is to talk about music. Finally he said, 'It's abstract. Words just don't do it.'"

Abstract? Was that it? And then, as I was mulling all this, Shirlbut came to mind.

A little earlier in my childhood, before my days in the rowboat, I had an imaginary friend named Shirlbut. She had braids like I did, but her hair was a little redder, like my sister's, and she had freckles. We understood each other perfectly. Shirlbut was shy, a child of the woods, and she needed me to look after her and show her how the world works. But one day when I was four, during a time when my brother and I were staying with our grandparents, it was decided that I should go to kindergarten. I was distraught. I knew I couldn't take Shirlbut to school with me, because when you are old enough to go to kindergarten, you are too old to have an imaginary friend.

We sat together in my grandmother's back garden. I tried to explain to her that I couldn't keep her anymore, but she didn't understand at all. I knew she wouldn't. We sobbed in the garden, high with August vegetables and hollyhocks, until I wrenched away from her and went to school.

When I got to the kindergarten room, I sat in front of a mean boy named Billy, who snatched my blue hat away from me and pulled my braids. I'd had enough of kindergarten right then and ran all the way back to the house. I told my grandparents with uncharacteristic emphasis that I was too young to go to kindergarten, and they relented. I rushed out to the garden for a grand reunion with Shirlbut. We were so relieved. And we were the only ones who ever knew how close we had come to losing each other.

Shirlbut was not abstract. She was a secret. She was vivid to me, and I could have talked about her if I had wanted to, but, except for the times she made me late or needed her own ice cream, we mostly hung out in a private world.

My transcendent experiences out on the raft were secret in a different way, I realized now. They were vivid too, and seemed profoundly real to me, ultimately real, but they never made it into stories that I told *myself.* They were more nearly the absence of stories, as if the foreground had been removed from me and I could see deeper into a living matrix that holds everything. Then, as I came back into my skin and rowed home, I turned again to what was going on in my everyday world. The quality of my attention changed, like a camera adjusting its focus onto what is at hand, and the wider view dissolved, not into abstraction exactly, but into something both invisible and implicit. I don't remember feeling either bereft or relieved when this would happen. But in retrospect I think I felt subtly separated from myself, from something I knew, something I wanted—separated from my own hushed prayer, *Show me.*

Surely an epiphany is the most ephemeral thing in this worldly world. "You can't touch its wings!" a child will say of the butterfly on her sleeve. And you can't touch an epiphany either, not with words. As the jazzman said of his music, words just don't do it, not because an epiphany is abstract (is music abstract?), but because it is so delicate. A person will speak of "moon" or "raft" or even "abstract" and feel confident, more or less, that anyone who knows moon or raft or abstract will be able to see it too. But, short of the poet who can point at things without hurting them, how can anyone hope to speak of consciousness transcending the body and spreading out all over the north woods and beyond?

Early on, we know the bind. An epiphany is supported by almost nothing on the street. The transcendent experience that seems truer than anything has ever seemed before will not be believed by this world. We hedge. "If I speak of it," we say, "I will expose it to ridicule, or diagnosis, or—worst of all—

the realm of the ordinary. If I don't speak of it, it will be hidden away, by me and from me."

And so the epiphany goes un-storied—more secret than a secret.

Yet without our stories, *all* of our stories, we are on shaky ground. The consummate storyteller Reynolds Price has done the research. In an essay about the origins of narrative, he writes that the need to tell and hear stories is essential to *Homo sapiens,* second in importance only after food, and before love and shelter. Storytelling is our urgent response to inner and outer events; something seen or known is "made visible in the telling." We ache to tell. Out of a primal longing for connection and confirmation, we say, "Look at this! Look with me!" And when we can't, we are diminished. And so is the world.

It is this sense of diminishment, I believe, that brings a client to psychotherapy. Other times, other cultures have been more hospitable to epiphanies. For eons, dreams and stories have been exchanged in the morning at the village well, or in song, or at night in the shaman's fire circle. The choice of a therapy setting, with its implication of "I need fixing" would happen only in a secular culture like our own. To this therapy place a client brings many untold stories, but the epiphanies are the farthest back, the most in need of rescue. This is not because epiphanies are inherently more worthy, it seems to me, but because they are the most endangered—these very moments when we feel most intensely alive and aware that *nothing needs fixing.*

. . .

ONE MORNING, a client of mine had been talking rapid-fire about almost unimaginably hard times in her family. Then—it was a mystery to me why this happened—she paused.

Her pause deepened into a silence, lengthened. Suffering had filled the room a moment before, but now her head tilted a little, and her face took on an inquiring look, as if she were looking *through* something to something else. Then a slow grin broke across her face.

"It's a miracle," she said quietly. "I'm perfectly all right."

What has just happened? Reynolds Price quotes the Eskimo hunter Orpingalik: "It will happen that the words we need will come of themselves. When the words we want to use shoot up of themselves—we get a new song." It was like that, like a new song coming.

The trembling moment hangs in the air. We can wonder where this "I'm perfectly all right" has come from, when there is nothing in the story of her life—or in the story most of us tell about where we come from—that would have predicted it. But that will come later. For now it is enough to thank everything holy that her all-right-ness has found expression in an ecstatic story, however spare, that becomes a new and crucial part of her self-description. And that she has found, for insurance, a witness.

My client's experience is important to those of us in the helping professions who do our work in the hope that the people we work with will feel better. But it is much more than that. It raises the question, If this moment is a *non sequitur* to what we thought we knew about a person—and about this universe we live in—what is the deeper truth? And how shall we make room for the new songs when they rise up from this truth?

To help make room, I undertake this book.

I offer stories of epiphanies as they have risen up for me, and as they have risen up for my clients who generously agree to share them here. Shyly we venture out with these stories into a world still in the thrall of a reluctant science and its cousin, a reluctant psychotherapy. Yet even now, as we shall see, science is encountering astonishing *non sequiturs* of its own, surprises that beg us to reinstate all our stories and include them in our explorations.

Above all, these are sacred tales. And they are profoundly healing as they remind us of—and restore us to—our innate all-right-ness.

SILVER BAY AND THE

QUESTION OF *I*

*Each of us inhabits two equally mysterious universes, one outside
the mind and the other within it.*

TIMOTHY FERRIS,
THE MIND'S SKY

A NEW CLIENT called me for help one day with a problem
that had taken him completely by surprise. He booked
the first opening I had and came into the office with a quick,
athletic walk and a firm handshake. He got right down to
business.

He found himself in a rough place, he said, caught up in an
attraction to a coworker. His feelings for her had come out of
the blue and had thrown his commitment to his marriage into
question. Leaning forward in his chair, he talked about how
the excitement of the attraction had seemed to rescue him
from a dullness that had settled into his life some time back.
But, he said, sitting back a little, he had a feeling that changing
partners would not amount to a real fix.

He paused for a minute.

Then, with an energetic motion of his hands, he erased the story he had just told from an imaginary chalkboard in the air. Hesitantly, he began again. "I don't think this is really about my marriage. I think it's something about . . . me. I can feel myself when I meditate and when I'm in the mountains. Something is alive when I ski really fast. But . . . *I* . . . don't feel connected with any of it." He emphasized this *I* with an open hand to his heart. "It's more like *I'm* watching. Now . . . this is weird . . . how did these *I's* get separated?"

What a good question, I thought. How did they?

A coyote in the wild will go eyeball to eyeball with you, run you clean through with a look that says, "I'm right here." So will a robin in the backyard, a cat in the kitchen. Sunflowers demonstrate their own kind of awareness when they turn to the sun, anemones close as the tide goes out, grass grows faster in July. Elephants mourn, and river otters joke around in the rapids. They are alive and knowing. But we *Homo sapiens* are the only living things we know of so far who can speak of ourselves as if from a place outside. Now and then it hits us— we see ourselves walking around in our lives, a little on the loose. Sometimes we prize this double awareness; sometimes we curse the day it was conferred.

There is a moment in laughter by day, in lucid dreaming by night, when a person becomes aware of the self who is laughing the laugh, dreaming the dream. It's a moment of surprise. Time stands still for a second. For a Tibetan Buddhist or an American plains Lakota, this moment is no big deal. But for a Westerner, it scares up a most maddening question: *Who am I, separate from what I do? Separate, even, from what I think?*

My client snorted an uneasy little snort. He looked at me expectantly, questions moving across his tan face like wind patterns on water. He smiled a crooked smile. And so did I.

I hoped he would forgive me for my hesitation. This *I* question has dogged me since my childhood summers on Silver Bay.

. . .

THE MICHIGAMIE RIVER runs through the woods of Michigan's Upper Peninsula into the Menominee River and the Green Bay finger of Lake Michigan. This is iron country, and the water—sometimes running quiet and deep, sometimes splashing along as rapids—is the color of pale root beer. At a point about halfway along its length, the river bows out into a graceful, kidney-shaped bay with a scrub-covered island near the shoreline and water lilies in the shallows. It is a place called Silver Bay.

Dave Davidson, a weekend fisherman from the Chicago area, came upon Silver Bay in 1926 and fished it for muskie, bass, northern pike, and rainbow trout. Back home, he gathered together some families from the Swedish Methodist Church in Evanston—Swedish Methodists were a rare breed—and proposed that they go in together to buy the land at Silver Bay and build summer cabins on it.

"It looks like Sweden," Dave said.

One of these Swedes was my grandfather, Brynolf. He and my grandmother, Lilly, chose the hilliest lot and built their cabin high among some birches, facing north out over the bay. The other families—the Davidsons, Petersons, Danielsons, and Johnsons—built low, closer to the water. Brynolf's was the only cabin that was red. His secret redwash formula had salt in it to help preserve the color, and the porcupines would come at night to chew and crunch on the salty logs where they were cross-notched at the corners, leaving their toothy signatures.

Every summer our family—in time, three generations of us—would drive up to the bay. Three generations, in young and old handwriting, would write in the logbook about horseback rides through the trees at the farm and time trials around the raft in the rowboat. Indian paintbrush. Beavers diving deep with a warning *Slap!* of their tails. Naps in the hammock. Three generations of us wore berry pails on our belts and made raspberry jam on the woodstove, skimming the bubbling syrup with an old wooden spoon stained purple. Swedish coffee brewed with an eggshell, every pot proclaimed, "Clear as cognac!"

My Uncle Dick would recover from his "war experience" at the bay. He dug earnest stone steps into the hillside down to the pebbly beach and built a long, wood pier in sections that rested on submerged iron horses and could be dragged up onto shore before the first autumn freeze.

Uncle Dick was a wonderful swimmer—he told us stories about bodysurfing in the South Pacific—and he promised us that if we would jump off the raft into the cold, root beer water, we would absolutely, positively come up.

"I guarantee you," he would say.

We believed the bay was bottomless, and if you drowned they would never find your body. We imagined our bodies, our flesh hideous and white, hanging somewhere in the gloom of this infinitely deep water. So even with Uncle Dick's guarantee, we would hug our skinny knees—almost jumping, chickening out, almost jumping, chickening out—until one cousin after another, one year after another, would take the hold-your-nose, risk-your-life leap, legs in the air like eggbeaters. (Everybody did come up, except Uncle Dick's wife, my Aunt Helen. She sank like a stone, and it seemed to us he had to dive a long way down to get her.) Once you could swim all the way around the raft without touching, you got to take the rowboat out on the bay by yourself.

Uncle Dick taught us how to shoot the rapids. If you try to swim it, he said, you'll get banged up, especially your legs, but if you relax, really relax, and let the water carry you along, you'll slip through the rocks sleek as an otter. We learned with practice that the principle was true; it was a swimming lesson, and more.

We thought, as you do in the wilderness, that we owned it all—these were our otters, our birches, our sky. We particularly congratulated ourselves on the fact that Silver Bay was the bay of a river, not a lake. It might be mistaken for a lake from certain vantage points, but we were always aware that the river flowed through. The sound of the rapids would come and go in the currents of the summer air, a subliminal reminder of the newness of the water, of mysteries upstream and downstream.

Wherever my family lived, and we moved a lot, we always knew that in summer we would drive, drive, drive until we were dumb in the head, turning at last from the pavement, to the gravel, to the two-rut road that led to the cabin. The tall grass growing up between the tracks whispered against the undercarriage of the car, and the evergreen fragrance of the forest poured in through the rolled-down windows. My brother and sister and I would cantilever ourselves into the front seat to claim the first view of the cabin.

"I see it!"

"No, I see it!

"I saw it first!"

"I did!"

We called it Up North.

FOR THE FIRST FEW DAYS Up North, we were bossy, city kids in the wild. We would smack mosquitoes and stand ready with the saltshaker in case anyone got a bloodsucker on their foot from under the pier. We would tell on each other for fishing from the rowboat standing up, because you could fall in with your clothes on and drown. Lightning could strike you if you didn't get off the bay right away in a storm, and there were spiders—you could be dead in five minutes—in the woodpile. We ran flat-out fast down the narrow path to the privy, day or night, especially night, because bears might ambush you on the path, and who-knew-what kind of snakes lay coiled in the woods.

Then, after a few days, we would slow down and slip into the world around us. Long summer days spread open and grew even longer. We would go for rides in the car at dusk to a couple of sure-fire fields where we saw deer in the alfalfa, and, on a lucky night, a mother bear and her cubs bounding with surprising grace over a fence, disappearing into the woods near where the berries were. These days absorbed us, softening our edges.

Back home, Up North was also an attitude, a meditation. It was what you thought about in a tough spot. "Think about Up North," my mother would say as she sent us off on subfreezing mornings in boots that would soon be full of snow. I would "think about Up North" right before a test on long division or in the dentist chair. I would close my eyes and take myself to the raft on the bay, rolling gently in the early afternoon breeze.

Silver Bay was more home to me than any other place. I knew every corner of it.

I loved this home in the wild.

And I hated it.

At night, everything was different.

> But who can I tell about nights
> when the road spills out
> from under my feet like water,
> and fear is all I know,
> the long fall to where words fail?

> Margaret Gibson,
> from "In the Desert"

IN MY BED at the loft window, I would prop myself up on my elbows and look out—fly out—over the nighttime bay. Overhead, the stars of the Milky Way, impossible numbers of stars, arched across the impossibly deep night sky from Cassiopeia to Scorpio. Arcturus, lying just off the curve of the Big Dipper's handle, was reflected in the bay, firing off every color in the rainbow. And sometimes, on a rare night, the ghostly shapes of the northern lights—pulsing to some magnificent, silent music—would begin as a glow low on the horizon and then rise up in undulating colors, almost to the zenith. The beauty of it! The immensity!

I would start to have trouble breathing.

I would gaze out and wonder, *How far? After the last star, what?* I felt compressed by my insignificance, as if I'd been whirled down into a grain of sand, too heavy to pick up.

I would say to myself, "*I.*" I would say, "*I . . . I . . . I.*" Panic building, I would think, *Who am* "I"? *Who was* I *before* I *was born? Who will* I *be after I'm dead? Will* I *be anything at all? Where? Is any of this real?*

I would try to back myself into the loft again, try to look around in the darkness and name the things on this side of the window—familiar people-made things existing in a different dimension from the night sky—to test whether they seemed real.

Dresserdresserdresserdresserdresserdresser.

Drawerdrawerdrawerdrawerdrawerdrawerdrawerdrawer.

I couldn't figure any of it out. My heart pounded so hard the bed shook. I tried to look to God for help.

OUR FAMILY RELIGION was called Christian Science.

Brynolf came upon Christian Science about the same time he was building the cabin on Silver Bay. It happened, my Aunt Catherine says, when "Grandpa met this woman who was a

Christian Scientist." I imagine her wearing a big hat. Whoever she was and whatever they said that day, it was a meeting that changed my grandfather's life and turned the family down a certain road. He—and eventually all of us—would be very serious about this metaphysical way of contemplating the world.

Mary Baker Eddy, the founder of Christian Science, grew up in New England at a time when the countryside was in flower with the writing of Ralph Waldo Emerson, Henry David Thoreau, Emily Dickinson, the Lowells and the Alcotts, William and Henry James. With the help of one of her brothers, Eddy studied Greek, Latin, and Hebrew. She pored over Plato, she wrote poetry. Gradually she pieced together a formidable self-education, which included a surprising apprenticeship with Phineas Parkhurst Quimby, a Maine clock mender turned mind healer. Born into a poor blacksmith's family, Quimby was an intriguing figure. Unlike other influential thinkers of the time, he had almost no formal schooling, but he seemed to be endowed with a natural gift for healing. When Eddy consulted Quimby about health problems she was having, he was helpful to her and a catalyst in her thinking.

Influenced primarily by the accounts of Jesus' healings in the Bible, but also by the transcendental thought of New England and by Quimby's idea that illness is mentally produced, Eddy spent the rest of her long life studying and developing her own ideas, radical ideas, about an invisible but all-pervading spiritual reality and the healing power of getting in touch with it through prayer.

She was fervently interested in the relationship between human consciousness and the ultimate realism of the sacred world. "We must look deep into realism instead of accepting only the outward sense of things," she wrote. And she urged, "Stand porter at the door of thought," suggesting—something more often heard in Buddhist realms—that a person can watch his or her thoughts from a stepped-back place or off to the side. From that place, a person's thinking or experiencing can be brought more nearly in line with what is really true about creation.

Eddy bluntly named her investigation "Christian Science," capitalizing "Science." This juxtaposition might not have seemed so striking if she had been working within an Eastern or shamanic or mystical tradition, where science, if it is thought of at all, is nothing more or less than the ultimate truth of all that is Real. But in nineteenth-century New England, the fiercely secular, little-s science—born in the course of the Copernican Revolution—was still in its ascendancy. The notion of a Christian Science that examined metaphysical questions—questions that had scrupulously been kept outside the purview of little s-science—puzzled and infuriated people. Christian Science was called an oxymoron. But Eddy was not proposing an adjunct Science that was meant to exist alongside science. She was proposing an encompassing Science, a qualitatively new, comprehensive theory of the universe, a sacred theory-of-everything.

I found the name of our religion a nuisance. What did it mean? Why couldn't we be something easier like Methodist or Catholic? I struggled mightily with the idea that what seems real . . . isn't, and with the idea that there is a deeper or more discerning *I* that can perceive the difference between the real and the Real. I memorized the Scientific Statement of Being, the central tenet of Eddy's metaphysics, and practiced it like scales on the piano: "There is no life, truth, intelligence, nor substance in matter. All is infinite Mind, and Its infinite manifestation, for God is All-in-all."

These were big ideas, hard for a child. They were strenuous ideas in the daytime; they were hell at night.

Summer days dawned on the bay cloudless and blue. Every morning seemed to promise that this would be the first day ever with no clouds at all. That meant good swimming from the raft. Then, by midmorning, flat-bottomed, billowy white clouds would begin to troop across the blue sky from west to east, and by early afternoon the sun was in and out, about fifty-fifty. I loved to go swimming anyway, and I loved to go alone. Lying on the raft, listening to the water lapping against it in soothing, haphazard rhythms, my mind would sometimes stretch out into metaphors and meaning.

I would think, *This is what Mrs. Eddy means. The sun is always there. The clouds only seem to hide it. The clouds are the transitory illusion. But*—and this is where it always got hard—*what is the origin of the clouds, of a person's "material beliefs,"* as she called them? *If God is All-in-all, where did material beliefs come from?* How to understand this?

Then the warmth of the sun, or the way the air was, or the sounds, or something more invisible than any of these—something would help me wordlessly. Occasionally and unpredictably I would really feel this All-ness. In a moment that was both calm and ecstatic, I would open out of myself or into myself—it's hard to say, spacially—past the edges of my personal life, past questions, past understanding, into a living place of unlimited dimension. There was no mistaking this. Something was there, making itself known, and *I*—different from my sense of *I* a minute before—was getting it with my I-ness. All-in-all.

But what is it about the night?

Up in the loft at night, I would come unmoored again. *There is no life, truth, intelligence, nor substance in matter.* This nighttime sky, this material world—the dresser and the drawers and my own pounding heart—it all seemed pretty real to me. I would try to bargain with Mary Baker Eddy. *No* separate *life, truth, intelligence in matter?* No. She was very tough on this point. No reality in matter. *It's a flickering then, a dream? But whose dream? And when I die, where will I be then? Anywhere? Everywhere? Thinking what? Who am I?*

My younger sister, Janie, was sleeping downstairs, a curtain away from Mother and Dad, and she was not sweating epistemology. But it turns out she was sweating something. "It was just something about Up North," she says now. "I would wonder why I am who I am. Looking at the stars, and beyond. What is a soul? What makes me different from the next guy? What happens when we die?"

Janie and I didn't talk to each other about any of it then. Under the awful night sky, I wrestled alone, bereft of what I had seen on the raft—these two ways of knowing myself not speaking to one another. Finally—after twisting around in my sheets, up on one elbow, then the other, trying, trying again—finally, I would give in to sleep.

In the morning, dawn would break as if nothing had happened, indifferent, it seemed, to the struggle. The early light on the mist rising from the bay was innocent, maddeningly cool. I would smooth the covers with hands that looked like mine. No evidence of hot struggle, no carnage. Chagrined, I would count the days left before we would be going home. I could involve myself with school and friends there, and if I sometimes felt hopelessly different, as if I were wearing an invisible Amish cape, I would at least be spared the northern sky from the loft window.

Then there would be sounds from the kitchen below, someone stirring up the fire in the woodstove, the fragrance of coffee. I would begin to think about the otters who had played hide-and-go-seek with me under the rowboat the day before and wonder if they would be out again today. I would sigh an early-morning sigh and wonder if I would ever make any sense of any of it.

. . .

I DIDN'T KNOW in those early mornings on Silver Bay that I would become a psychotherapist. And when I became a psychotherapist, I didn't know, not quite, that the work would be a continuation of this old, old longing to make sense of it all. But when my new client comes to therapy and says, "I don't think this is really about my marriage, I think it's something about *me,*" I find myself slipping out of ordinary time and space to a place I have been before. *I.* Out under the sky, who is this *I*?

"Something," my client is saying—I'm remembering the raft, water lapping on the drums—"something is alive when I ski really fast, but *I* don't feel connected with any of it. More like *I'm* watching. Now, this is weird. How did these *I*'s get separated?"

Yes, how did they? And what conceptual maps of a person do we use in contemplating the question? What conceptual maps of the universe? We could say that he is dissociating, taking leave of himself because it is too painful to stay.

But as he and I meet, one crooked grin to another, I'm tilting in a different direction—thinking about all the journeys that have been made into the land of *I* by mystics, poets, and, most recently, by frontier studies in quantum theory and human consciousness. These journeys are difficult to speak of in psychological parlance. They are difficult to speak of at all.

I ask my client if he is willing to be in a place of not-knowing for a while.

· 2 ·

QUANTUM PHYSICS
ON THE CAR RADIO

Something unknown is doing we don't know what.

SIR ARTHUR EDDINGTON,
BEYOND THE VEIL OF PHYSICS

D RIVING HOME for lunch one day, I was thinking about
my new client and about the clients I had seen that
morning, when a voice on the radio sneaked into my reverie.
It was saying something about a panel of physicists and the
eerie wonders of the quantum universe. I reached over to find
some music, when something stopped me.

What happened next made me pull the car over.

"If you think you have a firm grip on reality," the radio
voice said, "chances are you've never studied the quantum
world, where anything can and does happen. Time can flow
backward, objects can be created out of nothing. This baffling
world . . . so strange that even the experts say if you aren't
confused about quantum physics then you haven't really

understood it . . . hang on for a ride into reality more unreal than science fiction."

My own sense of time wobbled to a stop. Images rushed in and filled the car—water and sky images, wide horizons, clouds coming and going.

What followed was nothing less than a crash course in twentieth-century physics, delivered in the friendly form of a "Science Friday" conversation between NPR's Ira Flatow, science writer John Gribben, physicist Daniel Greenberger, and a call-in from Albert Einstein, portrayed with just the right phony accent. The essence of the course was that science has found, to its vexation, that while large objects of the universe behave according to long-standing Newtonian laws, small ones don't. As soon as it became technically possible for scientists to look into the microscopic realm of subatomic or quantum events, nature was caught breaking rules that had been thought to be forever unbreakable.

A particle of "matter," the panel was saying, actually seems to be more like a momentary condensation or concentration of energy than a "piece" of something, and it can *shapeshift,* manifesting as a particle or as a wave, depending upon the choices an observer makes in his or her research design. If the experiment is designed to study waves, matter behaves like waves; if the experiment is designed to study particles, matter behaves like particles.

These unexpected findings, they said, confound all previous theories of matter. More than that, they suggest a deep relationship between the observer and the observed never imagined before—a relationship so deep, so fundamental, that they can no longer be thought to exist in the world independent of one another.

Even more unsettling, the panel went on, is the "nonlocality" theorem of the Irish physicist John Stewart Bell, which says that two subatomic particles, even when they are separated by light years, can recognize and influence one another *instantly*. Bell speculated that the particles, however distant, are in instantaneous and constant communication with each other, not because they are "psychic" or "fast," but because at a deeper level of reality they *are* the same thing—only seemingly separate aspects of an indivisible, whole system.

This talk of Bell's theorem, which has been called "*the* most profound discovery of science," now triggered a call-in to the show from Albert Einstein, who complained in the fake accent that his calculations indicated a message can travel at the speed of light, but not faster, certainly not instantly. "What would you call that," he chided, "spooky action at a distance?"

"Albert," the panel gently informed him, "this is not just theoretical. Since you've been gone, instantaneous nonlocal connections have actually been observed and validated with the help of super-sophisticated technology." Spookier still, they said—Einstein still harrumphing in the background—quantum events seem to be able to go forward or backward in time, suggesting that time is more like a fluid landscape than a linear trajectory. Suggesting, even, that you can influence the past.

Pulled over at the curb, I sat transfixed. I was aware that I was hanging ludicrously onto the locked steering wheel, warping back and forth between the panelists' imagery and my own. I fumbled a few words down on whatever there was to write on, blinking away tears. These were descriptions, in a different language maybe, of an underlying universe I had always known. When did I forget?

I flashed to a favorite tale of mine. It was a mystery story that had been waiting in my head for an explanation—a story, I had always believed, that could change a person's life.

A friend of mine was asleep in his bed in Berkeley. Suddenly he lunged up and cried out in pain, holding onto his left shoulder. His wife, a nurse, could only guess that he was having a coronary. Crazily, but true to her nurse's training, she made note of the time on their digital clock glowing green there in the dark. My friend's pain began to subside, but the two of them, too shaken to go back to sleep, went down to the kitchen to make coffee. They sat waiting for the early morning paper to arrive when the phone rang. It was their sister-in-law calling from Australia to tell them that her husband—my friend's identical twin brother—had been thrown from his horse, shattering his left shoulder.

The wives talked for a little while. The accident, they realized, had happened at the moment of my friend's middle-of-the-night "attack."

I wondered. *Twin brothers, twin photons. If everything in the quantum universe knows about everything else and knows it instantly, do we begin to have a* scientific *intimation of how my friend simultaneously experiences his twin brother's shattered shoulder? Could the notion of nonlocality, which irked Einstein to the end of his days, tell us something about how far-distant brothers can be in instantaneous contact with each other? Could there be a quantum theory of human consciousness? A single theory of an intelligent universe?*

GRADUALLY, I BECAME AWARE of cars whizzing by. Through my windshield, children in bright colors were moving abstractly in the distance, and I saw that I had pulled over alongside a school yard.

As the voices on the radio talked on, a long-ago scene came to mind, a fourth-grade scene, when my science teacher, Mr. Emery, asked us to bring in jars of pond water. That meant venturing into The Swamp, a low place back behind the house where my brother, Dick, and Freddy Hutchinson mucked around for frogs after a heavy rain. Mr. Emery was Gene Kelly handsome, and I was crazy about him. So I brought in my jar. But I remember thinking that science didn't really have anything to do with me.

Mr. Emery used a small dropper to put a spot of pond water on a glass slide. He peered into our black classroom microscope and turned the knob to focus it while we got in line to see. After a long, fidgety wait in line, it was my turn. It took me a little while to get used to the eyepiece and focus on the slide, when suddenly I dialed into view a world I had not suspected was there, a world of transparent creatures swimming and spinning around among brilliant green vegetation.

At first these creatures all seemed to be going about their own business. Then, as I got used to them, I sensed that they were aware of each other and, in a way, of Mr. Emery as he was fooling around with them. He would add a tiny droplet of colored nutrient to their water, and the amoeba would glide over to it, fold around it, and slowly, slowly absorb it through its pulsing membrane. He would stick the point of a sewing pin in the direction of a paramecium who would shy back and then spin its legs and shoot away.

A moment before, pond water was pond water—swamps, and Freddy, frogs, and the family bathtub ruined by rings of my brother's mud. Now I found that I could travel through the microscope and enter into a liquid village of living creatures that seemed to be able to investigate, to interact, to swim toward each other with intention and swim away again. My mind swarmed with questions. *Could they taste? What did they think about? Did they worry, as I did, about dying? Could they see my eye?*

My experience of this microscopic world made all of creation different than it had been a moment before. It was relational. It was more than that. It was continuous, flowing both ways through the lens of the microscope. I and these tiny organisms were members of the same family, emanations of one great life. I had often had experiences of being completely absorbed in nature those summers Up North, but that was another world far away. I had not expected anything so transcendent in town, certainly not in science class. In fact I didn't think of this transforming experience as science at all. It was more like pond-water social studies. And of course I was more in love with Mr. Emery than ever.

Then I forgot all about it.

As Mr. Emery and the pond water experiments came flooding back to me there in my car, I thought, *physics* is *sounding like social studies. The quantum world is as interactive and continuous as my pond water. And subatomic particles* do *see the eye that sees them.*

My early religious studies came rushing back, too. As a child I had never imagined that science and Christian Science, each attempting to describe seemingly different realities, would converge. Each of these worlds had seemed true and yet opposite. Like the city and the country. The real and the Real. After a while the struggle became too difficult, and I stowed it away. Too hard. I had other fish to fry.

Now, through a chance encounter with quantum physics, I had stumbled across the news that traditional descriptions of matter are defunct. This news was not exactly hot off the press—some of these findings are already eighty, ninety, one hundred years old. But it was still pretty big news to me. Even the physicists on the radio were speaking with amazement and some chagrin as they talked about the subatomic "building blocks" of the material universe, which seem to amount to almost dreamy flickerings of energy that come and go in some kind of vast subatomic space or medium that is virtually "empty" and yet dynamically alive.

I was amazed by the possibility that my early experiences out on the raft, unspoken even by me to me, might become speakable at last. Was there really a conversation in progress in the world of this new science that could help me reclaim the invisible landscape I had experienced at Silver Bay? Nothing in my years of reading psychology, philosophy, or religion had ever quite spoken of my long-secret epiphany in this way, not even the poetry of mystics. These physicists on the radio were not speaking of one great heart beating throughout the universe, not quite, but they were talking about a frontier science that is contemplating a mysterious realm beyond or within—it's hard to say just where it is—the world we observe with our five senses. And it is contemplating this realm with expressions of astonishment, humility, and awe.

IT WAS GETTING ALONG toward one o'clock now. The bright shapes in the school yard were lining up at their classroom doors, as I sat marveling at these other images—observer/observed, curved space, liquid time. *Matter has been overthrown by the science of matter itself,* I thought. *Mind-matter-time, thought to be distinct, are so intertwined that they might better be thought of as aspects of one another, of something alive.* This was so familiar; I did not want to lose it again.

I thought again about my morning clients and their lives—an earnest couple trying to find a way to stay together, a young person tormented by skin pain that confounded his doctors, a premed student battling with a lack of self-confidence that had to do, she thought, with the way she was raised. Surely a person's most compelling problems or a family's most entrenched patterns, I thought, are no more solid than a seemingly solid particle of seemingly solid matter.

Yet we are still in the thrall of a stubborn empiricism. In this secular climate, the happiest surprise is an endangered thing. Even while tales of revelation are cornerstones of the world's great religions, we formalize them as myth and keep our transcendent moments secret from each other and from ourselves, not to appear fatuous or flat-out crazy. And so I sat in my steamy car, wondering: *What was I not hearing in the therapy? What surprises were ready, waiting to come?*

As the "Science Friday" theme music was coming up, Daniel Greenberger got in the last word. "And," he said in a hold-onto-your-hats kind of voice, "crazy as it looks now, the universe is going to look a whole lot crazier before we are through." Turning the key in the ignition, I realized I had missed lunch.

Something broke and something opened.
I filled up like a new wineskin.

Annie Dillard,
Pilgrim at Tinker Creek

ONE DAY A CLIENT came in for her regular appointment looking uncharacteristically fitful and pale. As I followed her into the room, I tried to guess what had caused the trouble that hung around her like a shroud. Something about her kids? Her husband? A rejection of her novel? A worsening of a long-time pattern of worry that had been diagnosed as an obsessive-compulsive disorder?

It took her a minute to gather herself and tell me. It was the week of her birthday, she said, and she had not heard anything from the family she'd grown up in—not her father, not her sister or brother. Growing up, she had always felt closest with her mother, who had died a couple of years earlier. After her mother's death, the others in the family had converted from wayward Catholicism to a fundamentalist Christian faith, and they had not been in touch with my client for more than a year.

"We don't understand each other at all anymore," she said in a tight voice, too fisted up against the pain to cry. "They think I'm damned, and there's no way they can reach me. There's no way I can reach them." She fingered the hem of her sleeve. "I've lost my mother, and now I've lost all of them. It's making me sick."

Her suffering filled the room.

I knew about my client's religious background, and on an impulse, I asked her if she knew the work of physician and author Larry Dossey. She didn't think so. I told her a little bit about Dossey's interest in certain nondenominational prayer studies that seem to show that prayer—especially "nondirected" prayer, like "Thy will be done"—has a positive physical and emotional effect on distant people, whether they are aware that they are being prayed for or not. It also seems to have a positive effect on those who are doing the praying.

"What is your prayer life like?" I asked her.

She was surprised by the question. I was surprised by it too. "Nobody's ever asked me that before," she said, looking as though she was not so sure where we were going.

"Maybe if we lived somewhere different, we would ask each other more often," I said. "Maybe we would meet in the road and ask, 'How's your love life going? How's your prayer life going?'"

"I never talk about it to anybody. I guess not even to myself." She studied her hands for a minute. "When I was afraid that I might miscarry, I said that prayer in *Frannie and Zooey*."

"Remind me."

"Oh, you know, 'Have mercy on me' over and over."

"How did you pray in your Catholic school days?"

"I said the rosary a lot. When I was thirteen . . . my father's heart attack . . . I would say the rosary all night on my knees." She paused. "My knees . . . I developed something, I think it was called cellulitis. The doctor said, 'Have you been scrubbing a lot of floors?'"

"What did you say?"

"'Yes.' I said, 'Yes.' Then my mother intervened. She said, 'You'd better stop praying all night.'"

"And so you did?"

"And so I did. I'm not sure I ever prayed again."

"If you were to pray about you and your family now, in some 'Thy will be done' way. . . ."

The room fell silent. At first, the silence felt like empty space. Then something about the air in the room began to pulse. There was a catch in my breath. I waited.

Slowly, she said, "Something is happening to me. . . ."

I waited. Something was happening to me, too.

Her hands were lying open on her lap now, soft. She was looking down, but I could see tears streaming down her cheeks.

"I'm feeling something wonderful," she said.

"Something wonderful has come into the room."

She was laughing. It was a sparkling, open-throated laugh that sounded like singing. She fluttered her hands and shook her head as if to protest this laughing. "What's happening here? This just came, didn't it!"

She laughed some more. Color was coming into her face, and her red hair looked luminous to me.

"You know, my husband has printed a collection of about fifteen of my short stories. I wasn't going to give copies to my family, but I am. Now I am. I see myself throwing paper airplanes over the wall. It doesn't matter what happens to them."

. . .

"THIS JUST CAME!" People have always exclaimed in the miraculous moment when something just arrives, telling us that what we're looking for is there, waiting to be found. Stories of these moments and of our efforts to make meaning of them are told all over the world. In the New England of the transcendentalists, Ralph Waldo Emerson wrote, "Everything in nature contains all the powers of nature. Everything is made of one hidden stuff."

One hundred years after Emerson, the widely respected astrophysicist D. S. Kothari joined this conversation about transcendent experience and meaning in a now-famous address to the Indian National Science Academy, which he called "Atom and Self." In his talk, Kothari, as much at home in the Upanishads as he is in contemporary physics, sounded as mystical as Emerson. "Is it that in reality there are not many minds," he asked, "but only One Mind?"

But a little further along in his address, Dr. Kothari seemed to demur. Speaking carefully about the relationship of what he called "cosmic religious feeling" and science, he said, "Transcendental experience goes beyond science." While it is true that human consciousness has a significance in quantum mechanics that has no counterpart in classical physics, he went on, human consciousness cannot be apprehended by science.

"This is because science is, by its very nature, incomplete," Kothari said—not incomplete in the sense that there is always more to be discovered, "but in the extraordinary and totally unexpected sense that there are fundamental truths about which we are intuitively certain, but which must always remain outside the domain of science."

Really? But if there is only One Mind, how can anything really be outside of anything? I am an old hand at this conundrum. Could there be a science big enough to hold prayers, and paper airplanes, and all our explorations? The thing and the understanding of the thing, all together? What sort of science would it be?

When my skier client comes into therapy to get help for an unexpected crush on his coworker, he stops himself dead in his tracks. "Now, how did these *I*'s get separated?" he asks, already getting an intimation of himself unseparated from himself. I ask him if he is willing to be in a place of not-knowing for a while, and we strike a deal. We will watch together for what comes.

One morning, after a few minutes of sitting quietly, he says, "Wait a minute. Something is happening to me." His eyes are closed.

The pause lengthens into a meditation.

"I felt this once before," he says after a while, testing the experience with words. "When my friend Allan died in a rock-climbing accident. At his memorial on the mountain, I felt so sad, but I also felt so glad to have known him. Sorrow and joy. They felt the same. Like kneading . . ." He makes a gesture with his hands.

"With a 'k'?"

". . . kneading, like bread. Folds in the dough. Sorrow and joy, inside and outside, everything folded together. And now I'm just feeling all of it . . . here." He held his hand to his heart. "No, wait, it's bigger. Actually it's bigger than I am. . . . I mean, I can open my eyes, sure, and see my arms and my legs, my clothes. But this extends beyond. . . . *This is what I've been looking for.*"

There is a vibrant moment of quiet.

Then he says in a different voice, "The only thing that could interfere with this discovery, this *feeling,* would be me."

"Which 'me'?" I ask him, realizing that we are back again with his very first question about himself—about the separation.

"The superstitious me. The one that tells me I'm not entitled to be happy. All that stuff I learned along the way about how I don't deserve it. . . . Wait a minute. I'm doing it again. Two *me's.* . . . But now I feel the kneading again. All these *me's* are me. All one piece. *I can feel it.*"

Tears are sliding down his tan cheeks. "Everything. It's all one piece."

WILL THE REAL REALITY

PLEASE STAND UP?

Reality is a slippery fish that often can be caught only in a net of spells, or with the hook of metaphor.

URSULA LEGUIN,
UNLOCKING THE AIR

M Y CLIENT SAYS, "Wait, something is happening to me." He motions toward his heart and then out beyond the edges of himself. "This is what I've been looking for!" Then he turns pensive. "The only thing that could interfere with this would be me—the superstitious me." Almost at once something threatens to wedge in, separating him from his experience again. He notices it and calls it an aspect of himself, a belief he's been carrying about not deserving happiness.

But there's a bigger problem. We live in an achingly secular period in human history. There is not much support in our daily lives for the moments of revelation that arrive, seemingly out of the blue. We are soon separated from them, or miss them altogether.

In earlier times, stories of revelation fared better. Europe during the "Dark Ages" was a countryside of people who lived lightly on the land and thought of the natural world as a continuum of their community and their cosmos. All of creation was alive and knowing—ladybugs in the pine needles, fish in the rapids, constellations of stars promenading across the night sky. Miracles were celebrated, marked on the map, passed down through generations. God was in every equation.

The world most of us came into was different. Reality was material, and science was the currency of the realm. This was a sober and systematic science; its way of knowing the material world was emblematic of a sound mind and a sound society. A ladybug or a pine needle was put together in a way that could be measured and weighed. Atoms and stars and the anatomical parts of a person obeyed the laws of Newton and Kepler. In my childhood, the study of these laws seemed to be for boys and involved levers and ergs, hydrogen sulfide that stunk up the halls, and creatures in jars of formaldehyde. As far as I was concerned, the boys could have it. I held my own mysteries close. Where would they go in the lexicon?

Then came the day I stumbled onto the conversation of quantum theorists talking on the radio about simultaneous events and things not existing until they are seen. This was a science whose imagery could accommodate those moments in therapy when a client suddenly leaps to a new and surprising place. Could quantum theory help us hang onto these moments a little longer, I wondered, and bring these epiphanies squarely into the therapeutic conversation? Could it *explain* them?

I wanted to be circumspect, but I ran, not walked, to a friend who is a science writer.

"Help me with this," I said. "These are the most overlooked moments in psychotherapy." If we knew how they work, I thought, maybe we would attend to them better. Make room for them. *Expect them.*

"Where are they coming from?" I wanted to know. "From the newly described quantum 'field'? From a place outside the current descriptions of science? Is it time to talk about the mystery of quantum phenomena as a metaphor—more than that, as a *mechanism*—for these moments of realization in a person's life?"

"Wait, wait. Slow down," he said. "Metaphor, okay, but mechanism? Can you justify the jump from subatomic to psychological?" He was not opposed to my drawing some encouragement from physics in thinking conceptually about leaps of the heart and mind. He was just not so sure that quantum nonlocality would turn out to have anything to do with these leaps. "Yes, the questions have answers," he said, "but can our meager minds even encompass them? Quantum mechanics may be a 'temporary expedient'—I think it was John Stewart Bell who suggested that—but you're asking a lot when you ask it to explain human consciousness."

I started reading books I would not have thought of reading before. One of them was an anthology of the mystical writings of the big names in twentieth-century physics, collected by Ken Wilber in his book *Quantum Questions.* Wilber, a scientist and philosopher, is not so sure quantum theory will ever explain mystical experience either. It's astonishing to notice that virtually all of these pioneering physicists became mystics in the course of their lives. But Wilber believes this was not because they found that physics offers support for a mystical world view, but because they found that physics can see only a partial slice of reality. Science is not yet in touch with an ultimate reality, these essays say, and so the rest must be left to metaphysics.

Still, I found that I was not the only one who was musing about the fluid comings and goings of the subatomic world as we try to imagine a "mechanism"—a clanky word left to us from earlier mechanical theories—for synchronous and revelatory moments. In my reading, I came across an exception to the collective view of the scientists in Ken Wilber's book. It was in the voice of Roger Penrose, the preeminent British mathematician, black hole theorist, and teacher of the astrophysicist Stephen Hawking.

Penrose, like many physical scientists lately, has been turning his attention to questions about human consciousness. When he looks over his own work as a mathematician, he finds that his best ideas have emerged not from a logical, deductive approach, but from sudden, intuitive insights into an "indescribably beautiful Platonic realm." How do we understand the creative capacity of the mind, he asks. How do we "understand" at all? Einstein had wondered about this too, but Penrose goes out on a limb. He predicts that explanations for how the human mind works lie in a yet-to-be-discovered physical theory that will reconcile quantum mechanics and relativity theory—a quantum theory of consciousness. Maybe something about microtubules?

Microtubules? Nevermind, I was glad for Penrose's company. I was glad not because I think we ought to rely on science to tell us where we are psychologically, but because I like the idea that there might be a science big enough to hold *all* of our experience. Maybe quantum imagery, with its implication that everything is known everywhere, can help us lay claim to our "anomalous" experiences with more energy, share them more easily, take better care of them. Maybe scientific conjecture can be an antidote to our skepticism about transcendent moments, the dark skepticism that says, "Isn't a person's subjective world too quirky or too California to have any ultimate merit in understanding the big questions? After all, where is the proof?"

> *We thought we were dealing with the world itself.*
> Erwin Schrœdinger,
> *Mind and Matter*

THERE IS AN OLD TALE, almost certainly apocryphal, that is told about Picasso. A man approaches Picasso at an exhibit of his work and says with great exasperation, "Why can't you paint more realistically?"

Picasso thinks for a minute and says, "Realistically. I guess I don't know what that is."

Frustrated, the man takes a photograph from his billfold and says, "Look! Like this. This is my wife."

Picasso takes the picture in his hand and looks at it. "She's so small," he says, and turning the photo sideways, "and so thin!"

What could this man do to help Picasso see who his wife really is? Bring him a life-size photograph? Too flat. A statue? Too rigid. How about his actual wife? But which one? The happy one? The one who is angry with him for going off to the Picasso exhibit without doing the dishes? *Will the real reality please stand up?*

This Picasso tale helps us see what I was beginning to see, that science has never been about reality, really. It is more like a knowledge tradition, a sequence of traditions—premodern, modern, postmodern—about reality and meaning that have been running through all of recorded history. These stories are tremendously persuasive. They have the power to confirm or disconfirm our experience, and they do it without our noticing.

I thought some more about my skier client, who had wavered for a second, almost costing himself his spontaneous healing experience. I recognized his wavering all too well. Ironically, these moments are at risk not only on the street but in one of the places one might most expect to find them: in the therapy office. This is obviously not because clients and therapists are not interested in moments that promise change. It's because of the secular tradition of psychotherapy itself, which derives from the science of the seventeenth century, still in its ascendancy in Victorian times when Freud was formulating his thinking.

Coming from this era, there prevails a psychological worldview that sees a person's life in the context of mechanistic causality, a view that runs the risk of disallowing spontaneous experience even as it prizes the realms of dreaming and the unconscious. *What were the scientific antecedents for this world-*

view? I wondered. I needed to remember what the science of the Enlightenment was really about.

I had never expected to undertake a review of the history of Western science, but the next thing I knew I was sitting on the floor with volumes of my kids' encyclopedia spread out all around me, each with little pieces of paper stuck in the pages. I made a chronological list of scientists and their dates on a yellow tablet—Copernicus, Bacon, Galileo, Kepler, Descartes, Boyle, Newton—and went to work.

Right about then, I made a trip that brought my history of science project to life.

I WAS DRIVING DOWN to Los Angeles for some meetings and decided to go the long way, stopping over for a couple of nights in Death Valley. The rainy season had given way to beautiful weather, and California was in bloom. Besides, the newly identified Hale-Bopp Comet had made its appearance in the northern sky, and I was dying to see it away from the wash of city lights.

The Central Valley was looking like a bride, with its orchards in full show, and in the Sierra, meadows of poppies and lupine blossomed as melting snow seeped in wet designs down granite faces. But on the east side of the Sierra, the sage landscape was drier, and in the Panamints to the southeast, the world was downright stark. By the time I was descending the long, mountain grade into Death Valley, I was starting to wonder why I had come to this place.

After the blossoms and snow-capped vistas, the naked folds of brown land shimmered in the heat—unearthly heat, even in March—and the high, bleached-out sky offered terrible comfort. A skinny range cow, all ribs, stood ludicrously in the shade of a telephone pole. Outlandish date palms marched along in planted rows at Furnace Creek Oasis, and glistening pairs of ravens, married for life, were panting in the fake-green fronds. There was an eerie hush over everything.

Death Valley isn't the real world, I thought to myself. *It's too still.* In the village area of the oasis, there was an occasional tour bus and the low throb of air conditioners, but the desert sky absorbed these murmurings of modern civilization. A few strides away from the settlement, the world was silent, as if the emptiness of the landscape blotted up everything into itself, even the passage of time.

Darkness fell abruptly, as it does in the desert. After dinner, I dragged a chair out onto the darkened lawn of the oasis compound. Right away, I saw it.

Rushing motionless along the black knife edge of the northern horizon was Hale-Bopp. My chair was cockeyed in the soft grass, one leg a little sunk, but the comet commanded my attention. Its glowing head and long, broom-like tail trailed along low and cool toward the sunset. It was moving, of course—swinging toward the sun in its big, elliptical orbit—and it was not. In this timeless place, the motion was timeless too, as subtle to the eye as the nighttime drift of the stars. I watched for a long time.

The next morning, a little before dawn, I set out for the trailhead at Golden Canyon with my daypack and some water. I wanted to hike up through the wind-sculpted sandstone hills, named for their surprising blond color, toward the valley overlook called Zabriskie Point. Two desert coyotes were trotting along the shoulder of the road. In the predawn light, they were more movement than shape—dancing, fading in and out—and I might not have seen them at all, except for their eyes. As I drove along, I realized that, like everything else, I was being absorbed into this strangely silent and beautiful landscape.

As the sun broke the horizon, the ambient light grew rich with color. The ancient desert lake bottom, which had been drab just a minute before, now became a haze of blooming yellow, purple, orange, and white. Each blossom of each plant—coreopsis, chicory, phacelia—was tiny, careful not to commit to more than it would be able to afford, but as I looked out over acres of these modest blossoms, the effect was of continuous color, pulsing and ethereal.

At that moment, my car radio, which had been giving off quiet scratchings about weather in Las Vegas, seemed to clear up, and a woman's crisp voice announced that on this night, viewers could watch a historic astronomical event. The unlit side of the quarter moon would pass directly over the star Aldebaran, the great red eye of Taurus the Bull, causing it to "blink." Aldebaran is one of those few first-magnitude stars that lies within the moon's ecliptic plane, and the spectacle of the star blinking off and on again occurs from time to time and can easily be seen with the naked eye. On another clear night, the radio voice said, exactly five hundred years before, the moon had quietly passed across Aldebaran in this same way. On that particular night, a young Polish student, Nicolaus Copernicus, happened to be watching.

I pulled into the Golden Canyon trailhead parking lot, congratulating myself that I would be witness to this astronomical anniversary here in Death Valley, where so little has changed in five hundred years—not the godforsaken climate, the smooth stone hills, not the resolute wildflowers or dancing coyotes. And yet, I was thinking that these eclipses frame a period of human history in which our relationship to our planet and to ourselves changed utterly and irreversibly.

Maybe the young Nicolaus whistled under his breath in the frosty night air. If others had seen Aldebaran wink out before, he was the first to comprehend that the bright orange star wasn't supposed to be in the ecliptic path of the moon—not according to the venerable charts of Ptolemy, not according to the entire Western philosophical construction of God's realm. But Ptolemy had gotten it wrong. Copernicus's singular recognition was the correction—the sun, not the Earth, was at the center of the known universe.

Cross-legged on my floor at home, I had been reminding myself of this tale. It's a thriller about men of the Church who blocked the publication of Copernicus's manuscript, a copy smuggled out, a published book slipped back into his hands on his deathbed by a loyal student. As things turned out, the dangerous discovery marked the dawn of a whole new science. More than that, it marked the dawn of a new epoch in human thought.

I laced up my boots and set off now, crunching my way up the trail toward the Point. The smooth stone hills and their shadows were abstract yellow and purple in the morning light, sometimes breaking up in the waves of heat. From the top I had a long, sun-drenched view. Death Valley and the mountains beyond extended as far as the eye could see.

The silence was complete. It gave no hint of time, or anniversaries, or intellectual history.

Many things that people had been able to see, people just couldn't see anymore because they didn't believe in them.
Pema Chodron,
The Wisdom of No Escape

LOOKING DOWN over the primeval valley, I drew a breath. As this rugged landscape lay timeless, human explorations of nature evolved dramatically, heralding a whole new way of thinking about the world.

Galileo turned the newly invented telescope toward the night sky and confirmed Copernicus's mathematical charts. Nature, the great mystical Mother of premodern times, became the object of a panned-back study that coolly restricted itself to the examination of "hard" properties of matter—size, shape, motion, and weight—according to what Galileo called the "scientific method." The "softer" properties of nature—taste, smell, color, and sound—resided "only in human consciousness," Galileo said, where they were not in the realm of "certain knowledge." Not science-worthy.

Galileo's cosmology proved to be too radical for the Church, and too arrogant. Tried and convicted by the Inquisition for heresy, he was made to recant. But it was too late. An inclusive new system of analytic thought was already in the making. Fractious to the end, Galileo continued his work in secret and died under house arrest.

It would not be until our own time that a papal commission of religious scholars would take up his case. In 1992, after ten years of deliberation, the commissioners acknowledged an evolution in Catholic thought and recommended to Pope John Paul II that Galileo be "rehabilitated." "From this case we can draw a lesson," the pope said. "It often happens that beyond two partial points of view which are in contrast, there exists a wider view of things which embraces both and integrates them."

From my perch on Zabriskie Point, I thought about partial points of view and a world changing. The telescope had revealed a universe more vast than anyone had imagined, and in the bargain something else was lost. In restricting its gaze to "objective" reality, science was observing a particular slice of the world. *And it didn't know it.* The rest gradually faded from view.

It was the beginning of a great forgetting.

I thought of Kepler, Bacon, Descartes, and Newton, stair-stepping chronologically through the period we now call the Scientific Age, each building on the work of his predecessor to construct an analytic cosmology of predictability and mathematical precision. In the end, it was Newton—scientist, mathematician, lawyer, historian, theologian, and explorer of the occult—whose elegant synthesis defined science for the modern era. He was a hero in his day, and his handsome science was expected to last for all time.

If the great Newtonian cosmology didn't last for all time, it lasted for a long time. The "facts" and "truths" of its deterministic reality comprised the mental architecture that Euro-

Americans lived in for three hundred years. It was a reality as invisible as it was pervasive, wiping out premodern sensibilities of a participatory universe. It became the filter through which people saw and heard and talked about the world.

Then, as the world turned into the twentieth century, the true nature of reality came into question again. Solid forms were found to be vast, empty expanses with atoms as occasional as stars in space. "Pieces" of matter turned out not to be pieces at all, behaving more like probabilities or tendencies-of-something-to-show-up, moving dizzyingly through curved space and liquid time. And the observer could no longer be factored out of the observed—not in the subatomic world, not in any world.

BACK AT FURNACE CREEK OASIS, the sun was setting. I dragged my chair out on the lawn again, watching as Hale-Bopp appeared, faint at first, low in the northern sky. Thrilling all over again, it flew in place, growing more and more distinct in the deepening darkness. A few fists away, higher in the sky and to the west, the other part of the show was about to begin. The quarter moon, traveling slowly, slowly through the "V" of Taurus, began to make its move on Aldebaran.

Everything in the valley seemed to hold its breath as the not-completely dark side of the moon edged alongside the bright orange star, hesitated for a beat, then overtook it. I half expected the lit crescent to bulge a little bigger or shine a little brighter, as if it had absorbed the star. Then Aldebaran came out from behind again—popped out, unfazed, unaware that this wasn't supposed to be happening, or that it was.

Death Valley *is* the real world, I whispered to myself. It quietly watches as the parade of stories about what is really real goes by.

> *Psychoanalysis creates an individual's past. History creates a society's past. To be comprehensible, each must employ a construct in order to simply manage otherwise unmanageable amounts of data. By making sense, history, whether personal or societal, differs from reality.*
>
> Neil Levy

A COLLEAGUE recently told me about a sister and brother of grade-school age he'd been seeing in therapy. Both of them had been sexually abused by their father and came to therapy only after he'd been court-ordered out of the house. More than anything else, my colleague wanted to cause no further harm to these children.

"You know, everybody has been talking to them," he said. "All the grown-ups—their mother and grandparents, their pediatrician, the police, people in the district attorney's office. Everybody is wanting to know what happened, how bad, how long. Asking for details, explaining, educating, reassuring."

I was trying to imagine the bewilderment of these children. "Sounds noisy."

"Yes. And you know, it's so interesting. Both of these kids were abused in a similar way by the same man, in the same family, during the same time. But it is clear from their responses to treatment that they've had very different experiences—filtered through their different gender identifications, different developmental stages, different everything. They make sense of what has happened in very different ways."

Therapists often bring difficult cases like this to their consultation group. My colleague did.

"How did that go?" I asked him.

"Well, you know, they wanted me to state my point, enunciate a theory, provide an example, and tie it up with a summary. We all want that."

We do, because it's a way of managing the unmanageable. It goes with the traditional and seemingly scientific way of thinking about diagnosis and treatment. Diagnosis: Here's what happened to these children then, and here's how it plays out in the therapy now. Treatment: If I do *this* in the session today, then maybe *that* will result tomorrow.

The English physicist and philosopher Sir James Jeans mulled the relationship of reality and viewpoint in his book *The Mysterious Universe,* written in 1931. "We are still imprisoned in our cave, with our backs to the light," he wrote, using the old image from Plato, "and we can only watch the shadows on the wall." From its observation of these shadows, science draws pictures of nature. After a while, these pictures—rough sketches, really—are easy to mistake for reality itself. Some of them eventually harden into belief, and they begin to shape what we experience and say to one another.

Psychotherapy does this, too. Wanting more than anything else to be helpful, therapists try to know. We have been trained in the tradition of modern science, even more than we realize. We believe that we should know. But can we really know what happened to this sister and brother? Can they? Can we know

what it meant to them then? What it means to them now? Do
the assumptions we make about what may or may not be true,
based on our academic and cultural training, help the children,
or do they compound the crimes that have been committed
against them?

．　．　．

ONE DAY A CLIENT of mine arrives uncharacteristically late
for her session. She rushes in, ashen and tight-voiced. She had
transposed the order of her therapy session and another appointment and was on the Bay Bridge going the other way before she realized what she'd done. "I'm absent-minded, and I
do these things," she says, standing there, shaking her hands in
apology. "But I knew I was keeping you waiting. I decided you
would think I was irredeemable and kick me out of therapy."

She and I have noticed that there are two stories—at least
two—that she has carried around with her about how she
came to be herself. One begins with her mother telling her as
a young girl that she was an unwanted baby. There were details
about a coat hanger. Later she suffered repeated sexual assaults
by a trusted family priest who played chess with her father in
the evening and came along on summer vacations. Neither her
family nor the Church could hear her tell what had happened
to her in her bedroom. There was an adolescence from hell.

Another story goes that she was a spunky little girl with
exuberant, curly hair, adored by her older sister and a favorite
aunt who often told her that she was quick and insightful and
blessed with a wonderful imagination. She went on long walks
along the river with her father, and caught crabs in Chesapeake

Bay. Secretly, she wrote poetry and kept it under her mattress. As an adult, she has good friends, is a colorful writer, and serves as a mentor to young artist friends. "Meant to be born," she says in a voice that comes up from her bones.

I ask her on this morning she has come in late, "What happens when we put ourselves in the story about being here on Earth, unwelcome and unprotected? From that place, what does it mean to be late for your appointment?"

"That's the place I've been in all the way here," she says. "It's terrible. I thought I would throw up on the bridge. I feel like I've done something so bad that somebody wants me dead. It feels fair that I should be dead."

She looks dead, she is so pale.

"And what about when we put ourselves in the story that you belong here? That you are here on purpose, and that you have a contribution to make to the world?"

There is only a moment's pause. I can tell from her face that she is changing the scene. Color rushes in, and she is alive again. "Oh! It's not a problem." She is laughing now, a lovely melodic laugh. "I'm only late. You used the time to write your memoirs!"

Which of these stories is true? The one about the "developmental arrests" she has suffered and how they might play out in our relationship? Psychotherapy can be keen on this one. The one about her native resilience? Which of her responses tells us about who she "really" is?

Old forms die hard. We still wear Cartesian divisions like a horse's blinders and see the world in the dualistic terms of a previous science: wave/particle, mind/matter, self/other, sickness/health, client/therapist. Physicists have to keep doing quantum experiments just to do battle with old mind habits, just to let the universe show them again how mysterious it really is.

How can psychotherapy, whenever it is tempted to rely on fixed templates for human development and wellness—on the tyranny of "normal"—be any less brave?

As my client and I shift from one story about who she "really" is to another, I watch her color change. These wonderings subtly uncouple the cause-and-effect bias of an out-moded science and, in the process, loosen our convictions about what happened in the past and what will happen as a result in the future. The minute we are relieved of the notion that a person's life is predetermined by circumstances—that it is something knowable, something fixable in a world of "well" or "unwell"—we are out of Plato's cave and into a living world that allows for three-dimensional surprises.

FRONTIER SCIENTISTS ARE TALKING about a mindful universe, located not in some geographical "elsewhere" but within this world we know. Mystics, too. From the beginning, it was out under the sky that I would feel it—something running right alongside daily life that reaches in, that bellies in and says, "Wait. There is more." It is these "Wait!" moments that arrive right in the middle of our struggles to make sense of things that make psychotherapy a mystical calling.

My client and I talk and don't talk, step on each other's words, fall silent. Then something surges into the room, bidden or unbidden, surprising us both—even when the problems of life are so painful that they take your breath away.

"Oh! It's not a problem, I'm only late," she says, and we are reminded of the radical indeterminacy of a person's life.

ISAAC NEWTON'S

NERVOUS BREAKDOWN

He walked alone, slowly through the silence,
with the sturdy and yet dreamlike walk of the orphan.

EUDORA WELTY,
"FIRST LOVE"

THE CONFERENCE that I was headed for in Los Angeles after my Death Valley stopover was called "Spirituality and Healing in Medicine," offered by Harvard Medical School and the Mind/Body Medical Institute. Health care providers from all over the country were gathering in a hotel ballroom called the Crystal Room, which features mirrors and an outsized chandelier. Fresh from my time in the desert, I was experiencing some serious reluctance about the crowd and the sparkles.

Dr. Herbert Benson, the course director and president of the Mind/Body Institute, opened the meetings by describing the genesis of the course and discussing the benefits for patients of quieting the mind. Over a period of twenty-five years, careful investigations had found that the state of relaxation—typically elicited by a repetitive prayer, sound, or phrase—was strikingly effective in alleviating the effects of a number of diseases, including hypertension, heart irregularities, chronic pain, insomnia, infertility, cancer, AIDS, anxiety, and depression. "In fact," Benson said with emphasis, "to the extent that any physical or psychological problem is caused or made worse by stress, the relaxation response is more effective than any other therapy we know about."

Then, in a development no one had been looking for, the research had found that patients experienced what they called "spirituality" in their relaxed state, whether they had used a religious repetitive focus or not. Spirituality was described as the presence of a power, a force, an energy, or what was perceived of as God, and this presence was experienced as *"close."* Nothing in the realm of medicine can claim results like these, Benson said, and it's time to bring these findings into a wider conversation about healing and spirituality.

Okay, I said to the chandelier. I'm here.

For the next three days, speakers from various backgrounds in science, spirituality, and healing joined in this conversation. Dr. Larry Dossey, editor of the journal, *Alternative Therapies in Health and Medicine,* talked about nonlocal models of the mind. Marilyn Schlitz, director of research at the Institute of Noetic Sciences, reported on the effects of long-distance prayer. There were presentations on yoga, and Zen, and Florence Nightingale. In a talk that I was particularly interested in, Virginia Harris, the chair of the Christian Science Board of Directors, told a story about a healing she had experienced after a serious car accident. Mary Baker Eddy's idea, she said—the familiarity of this made me smile—"was that matter is a phenomenon of thought. So thought is the patient; belief is the arena where change needs to take place."

On the third day, Stephen Kosslyn, a Harvard psychologist-neurologist, spoke about visual imagery and healing. Imagery has been found to be the most effective way to alleviate pain, he said, hands-down. Better than morphine, better than anything. Maybe this is because an image of a thing is as real to the brain as the thing itself. Notice what happens when a subject is asked to look at an image of a battered woman, Kosslyn said, as he projected a slide that showed increases in the subject's stress-related physiological responses. Now notice what happens when the same subject is shown a computer-doctored image of the woman. Now she is not battered, and the image is not disturbing. A second slide indicated a quieting of the subject's stress-related responses.

Then Kosslyn caught me by surprise. Even after the image has been computer-doctored, he said, "a therapist still reacts to the battered image." It was not clear to me what therapist he was talking about, or exactly how he knew this, but I recognized this therapist in myself.

Earlier, Herbert Benson had said that in trying to bring together the parallel tracks of science and spirituality, the Institute had invited clergy to Harvard. "But, we found that most clergy were so stressed in their lives they had stopped praying!"

Yes, I thought now, *they had forgotten.* Psychotherapists, too. Intent on helping, caught in the grammar of damage, we have forgotten what it is that helps.

For me, the whole conference came down to this—forgetting what helps.

As I was mulling all this over, Benson was bringing things to a close. Then, as people began to gather up their things and trail out, he made a last-minute announcement. "If you, or anyone you know has experienced what you might call 'enlightenment,'" he said, "we would like to talk with you. We don't know enough about enlightenment and its implications."

Amazing, I thought, taking one more look at the chandelier overhead. Amazing.

ON MY WAY HOME, I thought about my first encounter with mind-body experimentation. Early in the fall of my freshman year at Reed College in Portland, Oregon, I found a notice in my campus mailbox that informed me that I had been selected "at random" to participate in a research project of one of the senior-class psychology majors. I was new to the heroic landscapes of the Northwest, not to mention the heroic amounts of assigned reading at Reed, and flushed with all this, I was thinking about choosing a major for myself. Not psychology. Definitely not.

As I was calculating how to decline this nasty invitation, I was informed that "at random" is something like jury duty—you can't say no. Before I knew it, I found myself in a dank little basement room at the University of Oregon Medical Center, across the Willamette River from Reed and miles—so it seemed—from my study carrel, where I was working my way through the *Iliad*. In this basement, among dripping pipes, I was asked to think up as many words beginning with "w" as I could—while sitting, mortified, with my bare feet in a bucket of ice water. A Lux timer slowly banged off ten minutes. Floating ice cubes clicked against each other. Wind-window-wine-wastepaper . . . how many "w" words were there? I was getting panicky, thinking I was not being very systematic and fervently wished I were back with the *Iliad* where I belonged.

I never asked the psych major what her experiment was meant to show. I sat on a folding chair out in the hallway afterwards, dabbing at my sorry feet with a paper towel and rubbing some warmth back into them, wistfully reassuring them that they—that I—had not morphed into something rat- or hamster-like in this evil-smelling basement of higher learning.

Now, as I zoomed north with the fast freeway traffic, I muttered to nobody, "Harvard wants to talk about spontaneous healing and enlightenment. Amazing."

What is at stake is sanity.

Susan Griffin,
The Eros of Everyday Life

A DEBATE has long raged about whether the "soft" sciences, including psychology and theories of psychotherapy, derive—or ought to derive—from the "hard" sciences. Freud, who was investigating the landscape of human consciousness when classical science still dominated Western thinking, was on both sides at once. He said that he wanted to think of himself as a scientist, but in his work with patients he was in a realm of free association and dreams, hard to reconcile with proof and repeatable results.

One hundred years later, researchers interested in study-ing human behavior—a person's ability to think-of-words-starting-with-w-while-sitting-with-bare-feet-in-ice-water, or violence in families, or generosity versus selfishness in high school students—find themselves in the tradition of "hard" sci-ence and must design a methodology consistent with "objec-tive observation practices" if they are going to apply for grant money or publish in trade journals. "Whether or not you be-lieve that detached scientific observation is possible," one re-searcher writes, "you still aspire to as much experimental control as possible."

Meanwhile, from as early as the divorce days of Jung and Freud, when Jung was turning in the direction of a nonlocal collective unconscious and those mysterious connections he called "synchronicities," there have been those who contend that social science does not and should not derive from natu-ral science—that it gets along better on its own legs.

In this tradition of psychology, which explicitly rejects sci-ence as a model, "narrative" therapists Michael White and David Epston have written, along with other postmodern the-orists, that we cannot *know* objective reality. And since we can-not, therapy would do well to move on from those something-broken/something-fixed metaphors borrowed from the physical sciences by a psychotherapy that conceptu-alizes a person's problems in mechanical terms like "damage," "reversal," "breakdown."

Epston and White ask, Isn't a person's life really more like stories we tell ourselves about our daily experiences? Life as narrative. Definitely not hard science.

But strangely, both sides of this debate continue to base their psychology-as-science/psychology-as-not-science arguments on Newtonian models of the universe. All the while, the most riveting moments in psychotherapy are those moments of surprise and discovery that seem like magic, or alchemy, or something sacred we don't know how to theorize about. These moments arrive like a dawning. Or a pop. There may be a rush of tears, an exclamation, a slow grin. However they come, there is no doubt about their reality.

BUT WHO *was* Isaac Newton, and what would he say about these moments of discovery in a person's life? His own life is one of the most compelling stories I have found in my reading about modern and postmodern thought—worth telling, I think, for our considerations of science, and alchemy, and what derives from what. It reads like a tragic clinical tale.

Newton was born in a little English hamlet in 1642, the year Galileo died. Baby Isaac's father had died just before his birth, and he came into the world so small and sickly that he was not expected to live. When he was two, his mother married for a second time. Her new husband was a wealthy minister whose plans did not include raising a son who was not his own, so the child was handed off to his grandmother.

Some say Newton's rocky start explains his later "psychotic" tendencies. We can be pretty sure that his young life wasn't the bucolic picture we see in grade-school science books of "Isaac reading under the apple tree." Soon enough, his stepfather died, and Newton was allowed to rejoin his mother and her younger children, but it was only to be pressed into service as the unhappy manager of her farmlands. Maybe he really did sit in the orchard reading, and maybe apples really were falling all around him, but by now he was desperate to go away to school.

As soon as he could, Newton made his way to Cambridge University. At nineteen, he was a little older than his classmates, and quieter. At first, he settled inconspicuously enough into a typical study of an Aristotelian universe and traditional descriptions of nature, but news of the growing scientific movement that was being called a "revolution" soon reached him. Late into the night he would read Descartes and the chemist, Robert Boyle. Struggling to integrate old and new ways of seeing the world, he wrote notes to himself in the unused pages of an exercise book, notes he labeled, "Certain Philosophical Questions."

By the time he received his bachelor's degree, Newton had mastered geometry, developed the binomial theorem, and invented calculus. At the age of twenty-three, he had quietly become the most brilliant mathematician in Europe. In short order he received a fellowship to Trinity College, was awarded the prestigious Lucasian professorship of mathematics, invented the reflecting telescope, and worked out the physics of color.

But as he was completing an important manuscript called *Opticks,* Newton began to behave strangely. People commented that he seemed anxious when *Opticks* was published and was unnecessarily sharp in his defense of it. Then, about the time he was engaged in hot debate with some English Jesuits about his theory of color, his mother died, and he seems to have suffered a complete mental "breakdown."

This is one of the most striking stories in the history of science, and yet it has gone almost unnoticed. At the age of thirty-six and in the prime of his intellectual development, this brilliant young standard-bearer for the newly emerging mechanical theory of the universe—an inclusive philosophy that would dominate Western thought for three hundred years—withdrew from the world.

In feverish seclusion, Newton returned to his undergraduate notebooks, among them the closely kept personal pages he had written in the night, the "Certain Philosophical Questions." These pages, it turns out, contained his observations and wonderings about the mystical Hermetic tradition, the Pythagoreans, Plato, magic, alchemy, and the divine nature of the universe. Going without eating or sleeping for days at a time, he read, wrote, and stirred alchemical brews. When he reemerged—we can almost see him stumbling out into the daylight—his concept of nature had undergone a fiery synthesis.

Newton had integrated the Hermetic notion of a creative, active principle in the universe with his physics of an inert, particulate matter. Back in the world again, he discussed the relationship of his metaphysical views and his scientific observations in two public papers. He had come to believe that the mysterious activity of alchemy was direct evidence of a cosmos infused with God and was necessary for an understanding of what he was calling "gravity." Gravity was "a divine energy," he wrote, an action of universal attraction and repulsion that exists between all bodies in the cosmos—holding them, one to another—resulting in the action of the tides, the orbits of the planets, and the falling of an apple to the ground.

Then Newton advanced a notion that would prove to be too radical for the time. He suggested that atoms were infinitesimally small points of matter held apart by powerful repulsive forces. The total amount of this atomic matter, he said, was so small compared to all of space that while the universe was filled with *divine energy,* it was virtually *empty of matter.*

Much has been said about Newton's arrogance, thin skin, and ugly temper. But even paranoids have enemies. Hermetic ideas were thought to be "low class" and dangerous to the social order by the ruling bourgeois class of Europe. Witches had been burned at the stake, and Newton watched, dismayed, as his disciple and Lucasian successor, William Whiston, lost his professorship at Cambridge for his religious beliefs. Critics began to use Newton's own mechanical theories to attack the metaphysics that formed the deep underpinnings of his newly integrated cosmology.

Newton's vision of an ever-changing universe, with forms rising up and falling back into what he called "Chaos," was too quirky for the High Church of England. Spokesmen for the Church demanded to know how people could sustain a belief in the stability of church and state if the universe were in such a state of flux. For a time, Newton argued that it was enough to know that God Himself had created the world out of this mysterious Chaos.

But then Newton panicked. Or maybe he felt he had no choice. Fearing even stronger public attacks, he began to revise his work, expunging references to mystical and Hermetic traditions. Over the next twenty years, he edited and reedited his manuscripts, dropping out references to an "active principle" at the heart of the universe. From a paper called *Queries,* he edited out a particularly poignant sentence with an agonizing double negative. "We cannot say," he wrote, and then erased, "that all Nature is not alive."

In the end, Newton's masterwork, the *Principia,* elaborates his quantitative descriptions of physical bodies in nature—inertia, force, and action-reaction—in strictly mechanical terms. And as his two intertwined instincts about nature—the mechanical vision and the deeper Hermetic vision—were coming undone, he seems to have suffered, to the alarm of his friends, at least two more "breakdowns," followed by long, fitful periods of withdrawal.

WHO WAS THIS enigmatic man?

It has been said variously that Newton was the most brilliant mind since Aristotle, that he was one of the last of the magi, that he brutishly asserted the entire materialist program into existence. Of himself, Newton said he was a revelator like Moses. He believed it was his mission to perceive God's plan and share it with the world. At the midpoint of his career, he saw a universe in constant motion, slowly "unwinding." As one life cycle dissolved into Chaos, the next cycle would emerge. It was an optimistic view. Expect the Millennium, he said. Expect the Second Coming of Christ.

Newton's later self-censorship—more poignant, more ironic, and more complete than Galileo's forced recantation—has made it as hard for us to know him as his sanitized theory has made it hard for us to know the world. But his secret, handwritten notes of a living and yet immaterial Chaos read today like an epic prophecy of a quantum universe, sacred in its origins. And we can only wonder: If Newton, a deeply religious person, had not felt compelled to surrender the full richness of his vision, where would science have gone? How would we be seeing the world now?

. . .

A BIOCHEMIST, recently out of graduate school, called me one day for a get-acquainted appointment to see whether therapy might be helpful to him. He and his primary-care doctor had been concerned about his symptoms of depression.

He walked into the room with the conspicuous grace of an athlete. I found myself trying to guess which sport. When he sat down, he looked as though he would be more comfortable someplace else, as if he had been sent from central casting and the briefcase he held on his lap was a prop. He was not wearing glasses, but I couldn't get the idea of Clark Kent out of my mind. I wondered if he could fly.

He introduced himself a little abruptly by saying that he had been seeing a woman for some time, but he couldn't tell whether he cared "enough" about her.

"She's a good friend," he said, "but I keep seeing her flaws, and they scare me about what things would be like in the future. I just won't let myself love anyone who isn't 'perfect.'"

Balancing the briefcase on his knees, he put quotes in the air around the word "perfect." He said he'd been thinking of breaking up with her and trying to meet other people. "Maybe I'm emotionally broken," he said. "Unable to commit."

"Broken." The word startled me. I went off on a silent riff about the model of a clockworks universe we have inherited, made up of parts that can "break." And "perfect"? Was he already onto something, putting quotation marks around it?

While I was digressing into the seventeenth century, he said that he'd been taking Prozac for depression and Dexedrine for an attention deficit disorder since high school. He said he thought the medications helped him some.

"But I've always felt an undertow," he said. He emphasized this "always" with an exasperation in his voice and a subtle collapse of his shoulders. An image of wings without air came to me.

"Always," I said. "I wonder. Have you ever watched to see if there are breaks in this 'always?' Moments—split seconds, even—when you might be experiencing something else?"

He thought for a minute. "I was a gymnast in high school and college. I don't think I was always in this 'always' when I was doing my sport." He grinned a little at the syntax. It was the first smile I'd seen.

Gymnastics. I asked him if he was aware of what was going on in his shoulders when he thought about this "always." With the movements of an athlete who is well-familiar with his body, he experimented a little with his shoulders, going into an easy pantomime of himself slumping and then straightening.

But then, as if he were taking himself by the scruff of the neck, he brought himself back to his concern about his relationship. "It's boring," he said. "Not going anywhere. I need to break it off."

I was struck by the contrast between the ease of his physical movements and his tense words of discouragement. His upper body started to sag again. This time he noticed it and looked up, noticing me noticing. He decided that he wanted to try coming in every other week for a while.

A few sessions later, he said that he'd been thinking about lowering the dose of his medications. "I've been taking them so long I've forgotten what the world is like without them," he said, sounding like he was curious to find out.

We were talking more about the "always." He said he'd begun to be aware that there was "something else," often when he was doing something physical like shooting baskets or jogging. I asked him if he had ever experimented with meditation. I offered him one of Jon Kabat-Zinn's books about meditation and mindfulness and suggested that meditation might be another "place" where he could watch for the something else. He had been coming to therapy with notes. "Write down what happens next," I suggested now.

The next session, he sat down, squared his shoulders and—without so much as a "How do you do?"—opened a new journal. Without preamble, he read an entry he'd written after meditating one afternoon. He read, "I realize I spend so much time wanting things to be a certain way that I miss the way things are. I'm not there for them. Or, I'm there with an attitude. Things in my life could be better if I were really there for them."

With this we were both at full attention.

"You seem to be noticing something that you're doing from a place *outside* the doing of it," I said. "'Wanting things to be a certain way' from another vantage point. Where do you go to do this noticing? What is that place like? How big is it?" I was thinking again about Clark Kent and Superman.

"It's bigger," he said. "Much bigger. I don't see any edges to it."

He was quiet for a few minutes, playing around with this, while I was wondering, *Bigger than what?*

"I can actually take myself back and forth between the 'wanting things to be a certain way' place,"—he indicated this place with spread hands, something about the size of a basketball—"and the 'much bigger' place." He gestured with his chin, which was all he had left to point with, to show me the bigger place that seemed to extend beyond his hands in all directions. He paused again. "Actually I think even when I'm caught inside this 'wanting,' I get intimations of the bigger place."

"How do you experience these intimations?"

"They're inspirations. Like fairies."

Fairies! This was not a word I would have expected. "We've been hearing a lot about angels lately," I said, "but not fairies. I haven't heard anybody talk about fairies for a long time."

"I know!" His face was animated.

I was imagining fairies from childhood books—sprightly little green people who hover like hummingbirds on transparent wings. Spelled "faeries."

I wondered what his fairies looked like, but I waited. I found myself feeling tremendously protective of this moment and others still to come. Who in his world would get this?

Who would take kindly to talk of inspiration and fairies? I thought of his brother's children back east.

"Could you imagine yourself telling a story about these fairies to your niece and nephew? Or draw them?"

"I don't exactly see them," he said. "I'm not very visual. . . . It's not what they look like, it's what they represent—they're positive, joyful, magic. The cause of serendipitous events in one's life. Yes. I think I could tell about them, yes." He was looking especially broad-shouldered.

At the door he turned. "Not exactly scientific is it, fairies?"

I thought for a minute. "Did you know that Isaac Newton was an alchemist?" I said.

"No," he said, not believing me.

"That's how he got gravity."

"Why don't we know that?" he asked.

"We lost that part. Toward the end, he disclaimed the alchemy."

"He disclaimed the alchemy part?" he said, with his hand on the knob. "He had it, and then he disclaimed it?"

When he came in for our next meeting a couple of weeks later, he was looking a little dejected. He said he had left the last session feeling happier than he had felt in a long time, but in the past two weeks he had not been experiencing "that many inspirations." The schedule at the lab had been brutal, and the friends he shot baskets with were preoccupied with whatever. Then he stopped.

"Wait. Unless we count . . . I interviewed well for a job promotion at the lab. I was basically clear about why I wanted the position. I was right there. Then I called my friend—I hadn't seen her for quite a while. We went to a movie, and afterwards I told her about my fairies. It felt really nice between us. . . . I don't know why I was thinking I hadn't had that many inspirations. I guess I'm still getting used to them— fairies. Maybe I was disclaiming them."

I REMEMBERED SOMETHING poetic that Isaac Newton wrote early in his career about the tail of a comet. He guessed that because it pointed away from the sun, it must be made up of a rare and subtle form of matter that contained a mysterious force strong enough to overcome the gravitational attraction of the sun. "A rare vapor," he said.

Poor, poor Isaac Newton. Poor world. Once Newton's cosmology had been hijacked by Newtonianism, there was no more room for alchemy, or rare vapors, or fairies. It was easier for a person to think of himself as broken.

· 5 ·

MIND SCIENCE

When psychoanalysts spend too much time with each other, they start believing in psychoanalysis.

ADAM PHILLIPS,
TERRORS AND EXPERTS

ONE DAY, I got a telephone call from my granddaughters Molly and Megan. I was pretty sure I knew what was coming.

Molly began in the reverential tone of a six-year-old, which is what she was then. "Annie! Mommy's going to have a new baby!"

I had already gotten the word from the horse's mouth, but I didn't want to spoil this big news. "Really, Molly! What do you think it's going to be?"

"I think . . . it's going to be a boy," she said, sounding as if she had been working on it.

"What would his name be, do you think?"

"I think . . . 'Brian.'"

Brian? A little pedestrian, I thought, considering Molly's usually flamboyant way of naming things. Maybe Brian was somebody in her class in school. "And what if it's a girl?"

She hesitated. "How about . . . how about 'Harmonica?'"

Harmonica! More like it. But now the phone clunked around as Megan, age four, grabbed for it. "Annie, guess what!" she said in a pipey new voice she had recently perfected with the help of her friend Nicole. "Guess what, we're going to have a new baby girl named 'Megan'!"

Close by, I could hear Molly's horrified objections. "No, Megan, no! No, Megan. We can't have another . . . we already . . . you already . . . ."

And then Megan, holding the phone away, said in a voice husky with slow, dripping scorn, "Molly. Get your breath out of my mind."

MIND. WHAT *IS* the mind? Where is it?

Brain, we know. The brain is in a skull, or in a jar. It has curls and convolutions, and it's sort of gray. It has spare parts, and we only use 10 percent of it, or maybe 2 percent. It has a speech center, a Mozart center. Neurologists or neurosurgeons take care of it. A PET scan can take pictures of the brain of a person looking at a cat, and we can compare them with pictures of the same person *thinking* about looking at a cat. Brains we know. Or, even when we don't quite know—how is it that feelings, brain, and stomach all speak at once?—we think we know what we don't quite know.

But mind? "Fine mind." "Right mind." "You're out of your mind." "I can't do a thing with my mind." "What a sick mind."

"Get your breath out of my mind." Billions of dollars are spent educating, analyzing, stimulating, quieting the mind. What is it, this mind?

Laurie, a friend and colleague of mine, is able to "read" minds, or she reads something, and she reads whatever it is with amazing specificity.

One time, during a heady family therapy conference up the coast at Bodega Bay, a few of us in the audience shot looks back and forth and agreed that we were getting restless. We crept out, stole a couple of glasses of wine from the hospitality table in the lobby, and made for a quiet room with a fireplace. Laurie offered to give each of us what she calls a "hand reading." Somehow she uses the hand to see into the mind, but then again, she can do it over the phone. "I don't actually know how I get what I get," Laurie says with shrug. She's not being coy, she really doesn't know.

In my hand, she saw details of my early life I had never told her about, including that my sister—she didn't know that I have a sister—was born when I was five and that our mother was feeling pretty overwhelmed at the time. Then she offered to read the hand of a colleague, Joan, who was both intrigued and a little reluctant. Laurie assured her that she wouldn't be able to "see" anything that Joan didn't want her to see, and so they agreed that she would take a "look."

"Oh," Laurie said, a little shaken as she studied Joan's hand. "You had a very hard time of it when you were a child."

Joan was taken aback. "I'm the only one I know who thought it would be better at the orphanage in town," she said.

Laurie nodded. "It was bad. I can't see how you got through it." Then she brightened. "Ah, rabbits! You built hutches and raised rabbits in your backyard. They got you through."

"Yes," Joan said softly, astonished and deeply moved. "That's right."

WITH THIS STORY and others like it, we have a big problem. Ever since Freud—ever since Descartes—we have focused like a laser on the uniqueness of the individual. In the realm of psychotherapy, there has been an extraordinary emphasis on the value of developing a "sense of self" and an "autonomous ego." "Separation-individuation" is considered the *sine qua non* of growing up. All of this language has to do with the Western notion of a boundaried individual human mind.

These ideas are always in the backdrop of our daily lives, but as inevitable as they seem, they are relatively recent inventions. To understand where they come from, we have to check back with Descartes. The trouble is that Descartes, who's been credited and blamed all these years for the particular kind of analytical or logical process now known as Cartesian, didn't exactly use the word "mind." And he didn't exactly know where thinking goes on either, not with the certainty he was forever craving. Maybe in the pineal gland at the center of the brain. Or then again, maybe in the "soul"—a word Descartes did use—which "exercises its functions" on the pineal gland. But if the soul is *incorporeal,* as Descartes believed it was, then. . . .

ONE NIGHT, Descartes had an ecstatic dream that revealed to him that he would be the one to bring all natural phenomena together into a wholly new and comprehensive science. He was twenty-three.

Descartes never doubted this dream. He spent the rest of his life constructing his scientific system, bringing mathematics to his highly original work on optics, refraction, meteorology, laws of physical bodies, geometry, and anatomy. Before ever reading Copernicus, he achieved his own "Copernican" theory of the earth's movement around the sun. And, like Galileo, he spoke of a "scientific method" that split the observing subject over here from the observed object over there.

But Descartes recognized that if it is I-over-here who observes that-over-there, we must come around to the question of "Who is this *I?*" What has been attributed to Descartes by history and what is at the center of the Cartesian worldview is that this split-off *I* is "mind." Yet, Descartes doesn't use the word "mind"—not in Latin, not in French. And he doesn't use the word "I" either. He sits and sits, alone in his room, in search of what is irreducibly true about *himself.* At last, he tells us, he finds it: "Cogito."

Rejecting his body as too impermanent, too fickle to tell him the certain truth about himself—relegating the human body to the physical world of that-over-there—he decides it is the act of thinking itself, whatever the thinking is *about,* that gives him the direct, indisputable evidence of himself he's been looking for. In Latin, "Cogito, ergo sum." In English, "I think, therefore I am." But this English construction imposes the notion of an I that is already a little too separate, because in Latin—cogito—the *I* is imbedded in the action of the verb itself. Descartes also tries to deliver this delicate notion of the thinker's self-awareness in his native French, "Lâme pense toujours," he says. "The soul always thinks." This is still not about the mind.

And so remarkably, Descartes doesn't speak of mind. He doesn't speak of *I*. He speaks of the very soul of a person as the source of thinking. And where is this thinking going on? Why, in the pineal gland. Or then again, maybe in the soul, which "exercises its functions" on the pineal gland. But if the soul is *incorporeal,* then. . . .

Here Descartes seems to break his pencil.

Or maybe he just doesn't fit within the confines of his reputation. He seems to be reaching for something as large as today's cosmologists who are daydreaming about an overarching Theory of Everything that would accommodate the discrepant physics of the macro- and micro-universes in a way that isn't yet obvious. Or maybe Descartes, a deeply religious person, is reaching for something even larger as he tries to reconcile his pristine science with his own immortal Catholic soul— reaching, as his dream prophesied, for a science large enough to contain Everything.

Maybe Descartes is no more Cartesian than Newton was Newtonian. In the end, he is caught up in the sweep of the cosmology that is named for him, which holds that a person's certain mind must be turned upon a certain, clockwork universe if we are to have any certain knowledge of the world. As with Newton, we get Descartes' materialism and we lose his ambiguity. We especially lose the ecstasy of his dream; we lose his God.

Mr. Forrester: *How are you?*
Therapist: *I'm well, thank you.*

*Here the therapist responds directly to the first expression of the
patient's interest in her as a person. More traditional psychoanalytic procedure would address itself to the aggression underlying
the anxiety about the therapist's well-being. This would be dis-
couraging to a patient whose level of object relations is rising
and it is therefore postponed in favor of providing an immediate
response which meets the libidinal side of the question.*

Gertrude and Rubin Blanck,
Ego Psychology

IF DESCARTES WAS A PIOUS Catholic trying to work out a
compatibility between soul and science by looking at the action of the soul on the body, then Freud, 250 years later, was
a secular Jew looking for the action of the mind—the secular
successor to the soul—on the body. Looking for a mind science, or so we say.

Just one hitch: There is no word in German for "mind."
There are words in German for "spirit" or "head," but like
Descartes, Freud used the word "soul"—in German, "die Seele."

What was Freud's true intention? To understand this gi-
ant figure of the twentieth century, English speakers have had
to trust in translation. But Bruno Bettelheim, a German-
speaking Viennese like Freud, says that our English translations are misleading. Since his death, Bettelheim has been
having some serious trouble with his reputation as a child psychiatrist, but so far he is not in trouble with his German. In a
book of his own which he pointedly entitles, *Freud and Man's*

Soul, he laments the loss of Freud's exquisitely personal and poetic language.

How curious, Bettelheim says, that the authoritative but problematic English translation of Freud's works, *The Standard Edition of the Complete Psychological Works of Sigmund Freud,* should be coedited by James Strachey, who was analyzed by Freud in Vienna, and by Freud's adored daughter, Anna Freud. Yet, again and again, Freud's carefully chosen language has been deliberately mistranslated—"corrupted," Bettelheim believes.

French and Spanish translations of Freud are more faithful to him, but in the English translation, there are odd infusions of Latin, and the language becomes dispirited and arcane. *Das Ich,* the deeply personal *I/me,* becomes the distant Latin *ego.* *Das Es,* that region of the soul that Freud saw as "more extensive, grander and more obscure" than the personal realm, becomes the Latin *id.* And *Das Uber-Ich,* the "upper-I," becomes the coolly, if not cruelly, detached *superego.* The lively, interwoven layers of a person that Freud described seem to float surrealistically in Euclidean space like dusty pieces of overstuffed furniture. For all of what we get from him, we lose something. We cough dry little coughs and speak of object relations when we mean love.

It is left for us to wonder why Freud wasn't more worried about the damage done to his intentions, Bettelheim says. Freud spoke and read English fluently, and most of the misleading English translations were completed in his lifetime. Maybe, though a large English readership was anticipated, it was because "no one imagined that the small and relatively insignificant group of analysts in the United States could have the slightest influence on the overall development of psychoanalysis."

Is that why? A little European snobbery? In *Civilization and Its Discontents,* Freud was openly disdainful of American culture, which he saw as materialistic, shallow, and foolishly optimistic. Recently his writings have come out of copyright, and a massive new project is under way in which many non-psychoanalyst translators are working on a new account of his work in English. Perhaps it is the coming of a literary Freud.

Even so, Freud's formulations are still difficult. He might not have been looking for a science of the mind, but he was looking for a science of the something. Drawing from the scientific constructions of the day, he reasoned that events of the soul, like all events in the universe, must arise from something that has happened before.

Intrigued with physical symptoms that were hard to explain anatomically, he looked for causation. In the case of a peculiar symptom called "glove anesthesia," he speculated that the numbness in the hand was "hysterical," meaning that it was a physical manifestation of a disorder of the *psyche* that requires a psychological explanation. It must derive from the patient's personal history, he said—from her thoughts. And if these thoughts are not in the conscious awareness of the thinker, then they must dwell in powerful but forgotten scenes in her life. This vast, hidden landscape of a person's unconscious became Freud's solution to the problem of where the most mysterious human events *come from.*

The notion of the human unconscious, although he is often credited with "discovering" it, is actually not original with

Freud, as Dostoevsky's novels remind us. In the United States, Mary Baker Eddy's charismatic mentor, Dr. Phineas Quimby, was reported to have cured his patients' physical problems by putting his hands on their heads and explaining to them that the origin of all disease is mental. When people objected that children suffer from illness before they've had time to form mental beliefs of their own, Quimby anticipated Freud by forty years by proposing that the unconscious mind can pick up the beliefs and suggestions of others without being aware of it. Bringing these beliefs into awareness, he thought, makes it possible to understand their effect on the physical body, thereby alleviating it. "The explanation is the cure," he would say.

What *is* original with Freud—and what is problematic— is that he labors to bring the unconscious into the domain of the very science that had banished it three hundred years before. It is the only science he has. It's the science that disallowed Descartes' dream.

The majestic unconscious; positivist science. This bizarre juxtaposition is what makes Freud's work such a troubling paradox—a paradox that has inspired, shaped, bullied, and bedeviled the world of Western psychology throughout the twentieth century.

Subsequent developments in the psychoanalytic tradition soon challenged the deterministic nature of Freud's theories about the origins of illness, but the constructions of classical science, including linear causality and what it means to be "normal," remain in force today in the world of psychology. In fact, Freud's signal contribution—looking at human development through the cause-and-effect lens of the positivist world view—has so thoroughly permeated Western thinking that many of us routinely subject ourselves to the whispered question, "What happened to me that explains why I am feeling this way?" And under this quiet or not-so-quiet question lies a defining twentieth-century belief: I *am* what's happened to me.

The great irony is that Freud felt the need to ground his investigations into human consciousness in positivist science, just as Einstein and the early quantum explorers were inadvertently dismantling it. For the rest of the twentieth century, and even now, the "soft" sciences, in particular psychological and psychoanalytic theory, have been running behind the times, basing their theories on a compelling but defunct story about an objectively knowable universe—leaving us little room to wonder out in the open how my friend "reads minds" and "remembers" the memories of another.

> *Everyone remembers things which never happened. And it is common knowledge that people often forget things which did. Either we are all fantasists and liars, or the past has nothing definite in it. I have heard people say we are shaped by our childhood. But which one?*
>
> Jeanette Winterson,
> *Sexing the Cherry*

A YOUNG WOMAN, the mother of two children came in for an appointment to see about starting some therapy. She sat forward in her chair, everything clenched, and looked at me hard, as if to say, "Where would I begin?"

A nightmare unfolded over the next few months—growing up in a chaotic family, sexual abuse, chemical dependency, and, when she was a teenager, a heart-stopping experience of kidnap and sadistic torture. In a car. With taped-up windows.

"Too much . . . ," she said for now, bending over her knees. Sobs broke loose, as she struggled to find the words. ". . . Permanently flawed."

I breathed out. "I wonder how you managed to come in at all," I said.

She was calmer then. She settled back into the chair, and her face softened into a quizzical expression that seemed to say she might be willing to wonder how she had managed to come in, too. It became a question we would wonder about together in the next few meetings.

One morning she sat down and said that she wanted to tell me about something that had happened out on the steps after her AA meeting the night before. One of the men who was a regular at the meeting had stopped to ask her why she was avoiding him. She knew why, and, on an impulse, she decided to tell him. He reminded her so much of her father, a person who has been cruel to her, that she was afraid of this man. In the twilight he was tearful as she told him, and, seeing his tears, she noticed her fear of him melting away.

"So simple," she said to me now, with a shrug of her shoulders. "Of course he's not my father." She paused. "Even my father is not my father, not in the way I've been carrying him around in my head."

We stopped at this. We both knew big territory was opening up.

But I was still stuck on something.

"Back up," I said. "How do you think you were able to tell this person what you told him?"

She was quiet for a minute. "I don't know. I was just standing out there on the steps, and I was thinking . . . well, I just thought, 'I am not my history.'"

"My father is not my father." "I am not my history." Everything in the room stopped to hear this, the dust motes drifting through the slice of sunlight behind her, everything.

SOME TIME LATER she came in for her appointment, tossed her jacket down, and said without preamble, "Unharmed previousness."

"Huh?" I said.

"Something like 'unsuspected inner resources.' I've been feeling them this week."

I felt myself grinning.

"I talked about them at my meeting, and somebody asked me if they're coming from God."

"And you said . . ."

"I said, 'Give me a little time!' I don't know about God yet, but I see that I have a choice about how much wretchedness I want to get into."

Grinning.

"It seems like it would be huge, doesn't it?" she said. "Actually it's subtle. Lucky I was looking."

We were wrong.

Ram Dass

A CURRENT *Random House Webster's Unabridged Dictionary* defines "psychotherapy" like this: "the science or method of curing psychological abnormalities and disorders by psychological techniques." By "psychological," *Webster's* means "pertaining to the mind." This comes awfully close to making psychotherapy sound like "the science that cures the mind." A cartoon image looms up: A psychotherapist is poised over a neatly draped operating field with tools and techniques in hand. We peer into the area prepared for surgery, and we see . . . what? . . . a person's mind?

Conventional medical wisdom says that a physical-chemical lesion in an anatomical part of a person will cause disease. A neurosurgeon would say that a particular lesion in the brain will cause, for example, epilepsy. If psychotherapy is conceived as an analog of medicine, one might suppose there is a lesion of the mind that is causing despair, say, or worry, or road rage, and that the lesion was caused, in turn, by something that has happened, maybe a long time ago.

But we are living in a day in which matter, the once-solid stuff of creation, is thought by physicists to be something as ephemeral as a local condensation of the quantum field that comes and then goes. Running right alongside the philosophical crisis in theoretical physics, we have a philosophical crisis in psychology. If "matter" is up for grabs, what about "mind?" *What do we mean* by the words in the dictionary's definition of psychotherapy: "science," "method," "curing," "abnormalities," "disorders" and "psychological techniques?" Can we really talk like this anymore?

Could we ever?

A few years ago, my husband, John, and I flew back to Washington, D. C., for a pair of conferences. John is a family doctor who has always been interested in an inclusive approach to medicine and healing. Sometimes his meetings have meaning for me and mine have meaning for him.

Toward the end of John's conference, Norman Hadler, Professor of Medicine, Microbiology, and Immunology at the University of North Carolina, took his turn at the microphone to speak on the subject of "Fibromyalgia, Chronic Fatigue Syndrome, and Related Iatrogenic Diagnostic Algorithms." I was not so sure I would stick through this one.

Hadler began by asking the audience to please not throw anything at him while he wondered out loud whether certain physical illnesses were ever as "real" as we thought. I looked at John. Hadler's difficult lecture title had rightly signaled a challenging discussion about how physical illness may sometimes be a construction of the medical establishment, hard-pushed by tradition and by the insurance industry to come up with diagnoses.

Hadler reminded his audience that until the year 1700, all of Western disease classifications were based on the patient's description of symptoms. If you went to a doctor complaining of coughing up a lot of phlegm, he would explain that you had catarrh, which meant that you were coughing up a lot of phlegm, and the doctor would give you something for your cough that might or might not help.

Then, in 1701, the English physician Thomas Sydenham, who is credited as the founder of modern clinical medicine and epidemiology, said that it was not enough to listen to how the patient was feeling and then treat the complaint symptomatically. The duty of the physician was to find the underlying pathoanatomical *cause,* shifting the emphasis from how to help a person feel better to an investigation into what was wrong with them and why.

"What's wrong with them," Hadler emphasized. The focus on ever smaller parts of a person—down to microscopic or biochemical parts—and putting them back into working order still stands as a basic tenet of current scientific theories of medicine. "We're very proud of it," he said, "and it works once in a while."

I whispered to John, "Sydenham must have lived next door to Isaac Newton. Same time, same place, same science."

"Shh," he said.

"Now patients come in complaining of something," Hadler continued, "and doctors like us do the most dangerous thing American physicians can do—we take a history. It is dangerous because we instruct our patients as we do it, and we actively restructure their experience of feeling poorly. We ask our questions, never telling them which answers are 'okay' and which aren't, and in this process, we educate them to believe that there is something wrong with them. We even educate them to believe that the something-wrong is going on in the part of them that matches up with our particular expertise."

Hadler described a double-blind experiment carried out in Dublin, Ireland. A group of patients, who had been diagnosed with a muscular-skeletal disorder called fibromyalgia by doctors in the rheumatology clinic, were examined by gastroenterologists. Two-thirds of these patients were now diagnosed with irritable bowel syndrome, a gastrointestinal disorder. At the same time, another group of patients who had been diagnosed with irritable bowel syndrome in the gastroenterology clinic, were examined by rheumatologists, who diagnosed two-thirds of them with fibromyalgia.

"We have a very real nosology problem here," Hadler said, meaning there is a problem with our system for classifying diseases. "Either we are dealing with one multi-system syndrome, or we don't know what we're dealing with."

"To a hammer, everything looks like a nail," I whispered.

"Shh," John said.

Western patients listen closely to their doctors' questions and instructions, Hadler was saying. They watch *60 Minutes* and read *Redbook,* trying, always trying, for richer, more detailed descriptions of what's-wrong-with-them—what's wrong with their sleep, or their joints, or bowels. The doctor is trying too, looking for throats that are pinker than pink. Poking for "shotty" lymph nodes, tender points. Counting: more than six? less than ten? "Here? How about here?"

I whispered, "Doctors trying to help patients in league with patients trying to help doctors, everybody spinning in the world of 'what's wrong with you?'"

"Shh."

Hadler was coming to the end of his talk. Using a word we don't hear in the doctor's office very often, he asked, "Whatever happened to the patients' precious sense of their own *invincibility?*" The medical story, according to Sydenham, is constructed in such a way that there is no room for invincibility. And if the hallmark of "normal" health is a person's ability to handle the inevitable episodes of illness in life with equanimity, Hadler said, we don't even have language to describe "just-right coping."

I'd been aware of people leaving the lecture, but as Hadler finished, I looked around and was surprised to find that the lecture hall was half empty. John and I gathered our things and waited for a few minutes at the door to buy a tape of Hadler's talk. Next, we would be making our way across town to rest up for a night and then attend a conference exploring new traditions in psychology and spirituality called, "Where Inner Work Meets the World," presented by the journal *Common Boundary*.

As we drove along, we talked about why people had left Hadler's talk early. Maybe it was because doctors don't want to hear his cautionary message. That's what John thought. Or maybe it was only that people were tired.

"It's the same for psychotherapists and clients," I said. "We spin in the world of 'what's-wrong-with-you?' too. There are so many more descriptions of 'what's-wrong-with-you?' than 'what's-right-with-you?' After a while, you feel as though you'd better *do* something, unfurl some science that cures the mind."

I've lived a terrible life, most of which never happened.
Mark Twain

THERE HAVE ALWAYS BEEN those who were skeptical of a science that cures the mind. There have always been "alternative" therapies—shamanic and religious healing, the human potential movement, existential psychotherapy, systems theory, psychedelic experimentation, art therapy, body work, and many more. But, even with its "neo-" reformations, mainline psychology continues to stake its reputation, Sydenham style, on personal history-taking, diagnosis, and a therapist who's expected to put things back in working order.

Enter the *Diagnostic and Statistical Manual of Mental Disorders,* the American Psychiatric Association's compendium of diagnostic criteria for all the things that can go wrong with a person's mind. Or the convenient pocket-size *Mini-D* for ready reference. Here are the concrete guidelines that will help you make a diagnosis, complete with an identifying number. If your client happens to have "nonbizarre delusions (i.e., involving situations that occur in real life, such as being followed, poisoned, infected, or loved at a distance, or deceived by spouse or lover, or having a disease) of at least 1 month's duration," then he or she may be suffering from a Delusional Disorder, 297.1. Next, you will want to know which subtype. Is it ergotomanic, grandiose, jealous, persecutory, somatic, mixed, or unspecified? How many of the diagnostic criteria are met? Is it mild, moderate, or severe? In partial remission, full remission, prior history? And so on.

Ergotomanic? What is that? Nobody really believes that the *DSM* describes the people we wake up with, or greet in passing, or have over for dinner, but it is the way practitioners must describe people who come for psychotherapy. It is the standard for legal definitions about whether a person is competent to be in charge of his or her own life, for insurance reimbursement, for questions about whether psychotropic medications might be helpful. And, some say, we are lucky to have it. "There was no agreement about what was meant by a mental disorder," Robert Spitzer, head of the Task Force for two *DSM* revisions, says in defense of the system. "The *DSM* revolution made available, for the first time, diagnostic criteria that people could agree upon."

No. No, this is not revolution. This is counterrevolution. These are machine-like descriptions held over from old-science. They are not about real people. They are not about anything possessed of life. Six lymph nodes or ten? Adjustment Disorder with Depressed Mood, 309.0, or Adjustment Disorder with Anxiety, 309.24? How would the system diagnose a young mother who exclaims that she is "permanently flawed"? How about when she says, "It's subtle—lucky I was looking"?

What *happens* when we shoehorn people into these formulations? What room is left for stories about invincibility, declarations of "unharmed previousness"?

Ram Dass was one of the speakers at the *Common Boundary* conference. He told a story about a time earlier in his life when he found himself doing something that he now believes had nothing to do with healing.

"I was at Harvard," he said solemnly, "and one of my appointments was to the health service, where I did psychotherapy. I was a Freudian. In those days, that was *in*. When people walked into my office, basically what I saw were psychosexual stages of development. I mean I saw 'early phallic' and 'late anal retentive,' and things like that."

"He doesn't mean late anal retentive," I whispered to John. "He means late anal. Anal retentive is something else again."

John had already heard it. He stifled a little laugh. "Shh," he said.

"And then, immediately, the minute I got my category, I had a whole thing to do," Ram Dass said. "And there it was. I was busy curing people. And . . . ." He paused to sigh a deep sigh. "And in that role, I think I did incredible violence to many people."

IN THAT ROLE. On the plane home, I was looking out the window, thinking about the two conferences and about helping in the face of formulations about helping. "In that role," a psychotherapist has "a whole thing to do" with categories and "curing" that derive from the expurgated dreams of Newton and Descartes and the chilly translations of Freud. Definitely not revolution.

But then a moment comes when a young mother "just" thinks she is not her history. "Unharmed previousness!"—this is where the real revolution is. It shatters the old "first-a-and-then-b" idea that insists we are marked, perhaps even "permanently flawed," by things that have happened to us, things that we remember or, worse, don't remember. It suggests the presence of an ongoing "I am," somehow sturdy, somehow resilient.

Recently my client came in to celebrate her therapy and say goodbye. She brought me a painting she had done of two women sitting side by side, looking out at the world together.

"I'm not getting anything I want," she said with a wonderful smile, "and it's all turning out perfectly."

Silver Bay came shimmering into my mind. Or it came
shimmering into my somewhere.

"I feel like something is floating me," she said.

POSTMODERN
PSYCHOTHERAPY: THE FEET
IN THE FOREGROUND

A child in Samoa asks her father, "What is knowledge?"
Her father answers, "The nearest shadow."

KIWI TAMASESE

I HAVE A BLURRY black-and-white photograph of Silver Bay in an old family album. Through the years, the bay was photographed in many moods—wind-whipped, still as glass, flaming orange at sundown—and virtually all of those photographs are better than this one. What is special about this one, indescribably special, is that it was taken by my mother and shows, in the foreground, her own bare feet as they dangle from the pier.

At a certain point in his career, painter and photographer David Hockney began to include images of himself in a series of photo collage portrait studies. It happened first when he was composing a portrait of the British photographer Bill Brandt and Brandt's wife, Noya.

"As I was finishing this piece," Hockney says, "Brandt asked me, 'Couldn't you be in the picture too?'" So Hockney turned the camera back onto himself and pieced some shots of his own face into the composition. Now we see his friends looking at him looking at them. After that, he often included his feet in his photographic studies. We see them in the foreground of his portrait of Norman Stevens, in the study of his mother at Bolton Abbey, on the boardwalk approach to the Brooklyn Bridge, and at the edge of the Grand Canyon. They seem to say, "I am here, and this is how it looks to me."

Hockney was looking for a way to show that, although his images are "taken" with an instrument, they are a record of a person looking. He is explicit about this, and, as we find ourselves looking with him, we experience a little vertigo. We thought we were going to be looking at the Grand Canyon, but it is more complicated than that. What's happening here?

"It's about the world, yes," he says of his work, "but ultimately about where we are in it, how we are in it. It's about the kind of perception a human being can have in the midst of living."

Maybe my mother was trying for what Hockney was trying for, or maybe she was just fooling around. Whatever it was that day, you can see—you can almost hear—the water dripping off her toes, dripping . . . sending out ripples, and the captured moment is incredibly intimate. The bay is not the bay in and of itself. It is her experience of the bay, and she brings us to that.

Something is breaking down here.

To be noticing the breakdown, to be explicit about it, is postmodern. To be in the sensuous, dripping moment of the encounter and to *comment* on being in it signals a challenge to the idea that a person can regard reality from a separate place. Knowing one requires knowing the other, the postmodernists say. What had separated photographer and landscape, subject and object, is gone here, and new meaning is discovered in the unpredictable moment of the living interaction.

We live in the postmodern world, where everything is possible and almost nothing is certain.

Vaclav Havel

MY OLD DICTIONARY goes from *postmistress* to *post-mortem*. *Postmodern* is not there. It's not in my spellcheck either.

"Modern" is a confusing word that means the historical period following the Middle Ages, but it also means contemporary styles in the arts, clothes, nutrition, and so on. It comes from the Latin *modo,* meaning "lately" or "just now." "Postmodern," then, would seem to mean . . . how mysterious . . . what comes after now?

"Postmodern" first appears in a dictionary newer than mine in the phrase "postmodern architecture," which arrives on the scene in the late twentieth century. And so architecture was the first arena of thought where the modern was said to be followed by the postmodern. Characterized, it says in this dictionary, by complex forms and illusions, postmodern design is more fanciful than the utilitarian lines of the modern school of design, which were an outgrowth and representation of the no-nonsense modern (classical) science of the Enlightenment.

As invisible as it was monolithic, modern science was at the center of the first truly world-wide worldview, and it spawned a global technological community. Science achieved this—not architecture, not poetry, not music, not dance. These expressions remained more regional and more distinct, arising from local landscapes, dialects, and heritages. It was science that transcended it all, and then went out past the atmosphere itself to look back at our blue-green planet and photograph it, making the transcendence explicit.

Today, science appears to transcend even itself. As seemingly indestructible notions of matter, energy, and time fall by the wayside, we can only watch, rubbing our eyes, for what comes after *now*. The postmodern paradigm watches, trying—like fingers caught in a Chinese finger catcher—to pull itself free from all paradigms. This is not so easy to do.

A friend teases, "You mean we can't even say, 'I am certain of the truth of this postmodern thinking?'"

Nope. Not even that. Nothing is a sure bet.

Vaclav Havel, who, together with his native Czechoslovakia, endured the tortures of totalitarian Nazi and Soviet occupations, celebrates the breakdown. He says his favorite symbol of postmodernism is a billboard of a Bedouin on a camel in the desert, with jeans peeking out from under his traditional robes. In his hand he holds a transistor radio, and on the camel's back there is a blanket bearing a woven black-on-red Coca-Cola insignia.

This is a complex, multicultural collage. It signals the collapse of an ancient way of living as it announces the arrival of new images and products delivered to remote places in the fast, global spread of multinational corporations. Good news? An ominous foreboding of political and economic exploitation? From the picture, we don't know.

A television commercial for Honda, a straight steal from meteorologist Edward Lorenz's "Butterfly Effect" theory of chaos and complexity in nature, presents another complex image of a postmodern world. The voice-over says that the beating of a butterfly's wings in faraway Malaysia (here's the butterfly, here's an exotic jungle scene) stirs the air, contributing to a gathering weather system that grows into a rainstorm strong enough to knock out the electricity in New Jersey, where a wet-haired young mother kisses her children goodbye and pulls out onto the slippery street, driving off to work in her trusty Civic. She might plug her Chinese-made hairdryer into her cigarette lighter and turn up the news from the BBC. We don't know. Anything seems possible.

Breakdowns. Blendings. Strange juxtapositions.

As the concept of postmodernism widens into something that is being called the postmodern mind, it begins to suggest our own constantly changing subjective experience, multiple vantage points, ambiguous meanings. David Hockney deals with this aspect of postmodernism too, when he plays with perspective in his painted landscapes, suggesting the optical parallax of our eyes. The farmhouse seems to get bigger as we get "closer," our eyes moving down the painted road.

The conversation is about how we construe a thing, or, in postmodern language—curiously mechanistic—how we "deconstruct" a thing. It is the person doing the noticing who is more reliable now, more "real," than the landscape itself. My mother, her feet dripping in the foreground, the Bedouin on the camel, the young woman in the Civic—we ourselves are the ones who are noticing and making meaning of everything that is going on. Everything that may be going on. We are the only part of the picture we can be certain of.

But can we be certain of ourselves? We are back to the question: Who are we, anyway? How would theories of psychotherapy address this perennial question?

and I thought
I am so many!
What is my name?

Mary Oliver,
from "Sunrise"

IN THE WORLD of psychotherapy, there have been two main, and sometimes antagonistic, camps of theorists.

There have been those practitioners, usually psychodynamic in their orientation, who have treated individual patients with the assumption that something is wrong with them or with the way they are going about things, which has its origins in their personal histories. This is still what a lot of people imagine when they think about psychotherapy and its Freudian origins. Often enough, a person will make a protective gesture somewhere around his or her head as if to say, "Don't look in here, it's a mess!"

Then, there have been family therapists who think the lens of the camera must be opened wider; they see individuals or families in therapy with the idea that the problem is not located in the personality of an individual but in the interactions of the "system" as a whole—the family, the community, the hierarchical culture. These systems theorists, working in the newer and less well-known tradition of cybernetics or information theory, want to know what else is going on.

"Open the lens wider," they say. "What else? Who else?" And so context or *ecology*—a word that had not been used in psychology before—is everything. "Stamp out nouns!" Gregory Bateson said, after hanging out with dolphin families. It's all in the verbs. A person is part of a complex, dynamic process; everything is in the action and interaction.

Virginia Satir, Bateson, and others at the Mental Research Institute of Palo Alto noticed that they could help a schizophrenic child in the hospital and send him home, only to find him returning in the same fix a few hours or a few days later. Maybe something in the family was wrong. They conjectured that the mother's communication pattern might be convoluted in a crazy-making way. A formula for a crazy-making admonition to the child might be: "Don't do that or else" + "Don't *not* do that or else" + "We're not going to talk about any of this." The child, in ghastly collaboration with the "schizophrenogenic" mother (and, some thought to add, the absent father), comprised a sick *system,* and the child was carrying the symptoms on behalf of the whole family.

In these readings of both psychodynamic and cybernetic theory—theories that resided in distinctly different journals and training institutions—something was wrong and needed to be fixed. The keeper of the symptoms—the person or the larger family system—had generated the presenting problem over time and was now in the habit of it, or was "needing" it to maintain a certain equilibrium. It was this unholy homeostasis that the therapist was meant to disrupt, like rebreaking a bone that has mended badly.

But as physical scientists were saying they were not so sure they knew what the world was, the separate camps of psychotherapists began to say they were not so sure they knew what a person was either.

Otto Kernberg talked about the "self." He speculated that a "normal" person is aware of a constant "self" that threads through all of her other selves—artist-mother-teacher-daughter—while a person with a "borderline personality disorder" is missing that awareness. But other theorists said maybe there is no certain "self." Maybe the self is something fluid, generated moment to moment in the interactions of relationship. Donald Winnicott, pointing to the embrace of a mother and infant, said there is no such thing as a baby. Jean Baker Miller and others at Wellesley's Stone Center said maybe there's no such thing as a grown-up either. Maybe "self" is an interactive improvisation, a chameleon sort of thing that changes colors according to its surroundings. Still others asked, "Then who are you when you go off alone?"

"There is no such thing as a person," family therapist Carl Whitaker emphatically said. "It's just a word for a fragment of the family." He refused to treat individual clients and loved to tell the story about the time he agreed, against his better judgment, to see a man who complained of impotence in individual therapy, only to discover that the man's wife, out in the waiting room, was not fond of sex. If there is no such thing as a person, maybe there is no such thing as a therapist, either, and Whitaker preferred to work with a co-therapist, sometimes his wife. "Hold onto my heels, I'm going in!" he would say to Muriel. He would say this for a laugh, but he was serious about trying to find a way to join the family and pick up the problem from inside the belly of it.

So what is it that happens in therapy?

Heinz Kohut, the author of a theory of therapy that has come to be called "Self Psychology," suggested that the therapist lends the patient certain psychological functions—the ability to connect with others, for example. At such a moment the patient is not quite a person, Kohut said. He is something more like a person-in-a-state-of-becoming who practices using these functions, borrowed in the therapy, as if they were his own.

Joseph Weiss and Harold Sampson, the authors of a theory they call "Control Mastery," say that patients come to therapy with certain "pathogenic beliefs." An example of a pathogenic belief might be, "If I am a success in the world, the tie between me and my father will be endangered." The patient "uses" the therapist to confirm or disconfirm the belief through "tests" the therapist passes (resulting in improvement, liveliness, clarity) or fails (resulting in deadening, compliance, diffuseness). The therapist doesn't have to know what the test is or what he must do to pass or fail in order to be "effective," Weiss and Sampson say. He just needs to pass it by hook or by crook, for the curative action to work.

But what is the curative action? And where? There is talk here of "practicing," of "tests." But when Weiss or Sampson passes the test, what happens? What happens when Whitaker "goes in"? When the psychoanalyst Elizabeth Mayer reports smelling fresh peaches a few seconds before her patient mentions that her father calls her his "Georgia peach"—what's happening there? Practitioners of both individual and family therapy watch with a mixture of excitement and dismay as postmodern questions explode all around us, including the most humbling questions about what a "self" might be and what a therapist is supposed to do or does.

· · ·

ONE OCTOBER FRIDAY AFTERNOON, I drove up to the Napa Valley for the annual weekend conference of my favorite professional organization, the Northern California Association of Family Therapists. Every year we assemble to catch up with each other and hear the latest in the theory and practice of family therapy. This time the presenter was going to be Michael White, an Australian "narrative" therapist who would be speaking about "Opening Space for the Performance of Alternative Knowledges."

The Napa Valley is beautiful in October. The leaves are scarlet and purple, the husky perfume of just-picked grapes hangs in the autumn air, the sky is blue and deep. But I sat down for the evening session next to my friend Jane, feeling Friday-night tired, distracted, and more than grumpy about missing the A's-Dodgers World Series game. Who knew what "opening space for the performance of alternative knowledges" might mean? Who cared? I hitched around in my seat, looking for the best escape route through the folding chairs to the back doors and the nearest TV.

There were other Friday night fidgeters too, but White, who should have been jet-lagged, was getting right down to it.

"Maps," he began, "inform the questions we ask in therapy."

Jane and I elbowed each other. We'd had lots of conversations about maps. Jane was one of my first and best teachers, and she is always ahead of me.

"You're not suggesting that we stop addressing developmental issues, are you?" I would ask her. "Don't you think it's helpful to get a history that provides a context for a person's pain and for how they're making sense of things?"

"Do it, sure," she would say. "Get the natural history of the problem, but remember, the map is not the territory."

Now White was saying, "Since we cannot know objective reality, all knowing amounts to an act of interpretation."

My mind sat up. I got out my notebook.

White continued. If we draw our analogies from the physical sciences—he meant the classical or "modern" physical sciences—we will tend to see problems presented in therapy as "breakdowns" or as developmental insufficiencies inherent in a person's character structure. From this vantage point, the therapist tries to diagnose and repair or reconstruct, according to certain theories or doctrines about maturity and wellness. "This," said White in his Australian lilt, "puts a painful burden on an 'expert' therapist."

I sighed. Even feminist formulations that had recognized the interdependence of researcher and subject for some time—and that objected to certain so-called hallmarks of human maturity, such as "autonomous," "independent," and "separate," on the grounds that they were sexist—still referred to "therapy" in terms of "something wrong" and "how to fix it." I was always worrying about the political implications of this. It meant that I, the leery champion of "wellness," was in a hierarchical relationship with my client, pretending that I lived more in the world of "well" than she did. At least, on a good day, I worried; on a bad day, the concern was out of my awareness.

But White had been reading the French postmodern philosopher Michel Foucault and the ethnographer Edward Bruner, who'd been working with native North Americans. White was playing around with ideas about the social "construction" of knowledge. If the therapist draws analogies from the metaphor of narrative instead of (old) science, he was saying, a client's problem can be construed or "deconstructed" as a story and "externalized."

Now the person (whatever a person is) can be separated from the problem. Instead of asking, "How long have you had this problem?" one can ask, "How long has this problem been pushing you around? How has it been interfering with the way you prefer to live your life?"

This notion of narrative is not about introducing an ideology, White insisted, but about exposing ideology. A distinction can be made between what a person's life is like and what the "dominant" cultural story may have to say about what a person's life is *supposed* to be like. The therapist serves as a partner in protest, inviting clients to think of times when they have not cooperated with the identified problem or with oppressive cultural "specifications" for personhood that may aid and abet the problem.

And in every person's life, White said, "there is always a history of protest. Always."

The language was difficult, but who doesn't love the idea of protest and liberation?

White went on. Once the dominant story has been challenged, there is an opening of space in the therapy room. Now the client can begin to get in touch with spontaneous experiences and preferred ways of being that originate in the moment of the therapy or are retrieved from a forgotten time. Themes of self-respect and personal courage can emerge, themes that have been invisible or forgotten since the person became submerged in the dominant story. Now the client and the therapist can explore ways of elaborating these newly discovered or rediscovered self-descriptions. Even where there has been child abuse, White said, a child has a treasure trove of experience—other stories already onboard—that can be made explicit, opening the way for a richer kind of self-reflection.

That night, I got the baseball score on the eleven o'clock news—Dodgers 5, A's 4—and spent the rest of the weekend listening to White, buzzing with friends, and going off on walks in the autumn colors to think things over. I thought about the fix-it mandate that weighed on me in my work, even when it was softened by relational or feminist theory or by my own metaphysical leanings. I talked with Jane about the politics of separating person and problem and about a theory that acknowledges the dicey postmodern questions about what a "self" is and then finesses them, turning its attention to the interaction between a person and his or her *stories* about being a person.

· · ·

A MAN CALLED for an appointment at the suggestion of his minister. When he came in, he was taller than I had imagined him on the phone, all arms and legs. He folded himself into the chair and introduced himself by saying that he had probably worried his minister when he had told her in confidence how discouraged and depressed he'd been.

"I think she was surprised," he said.

"Why, do you suppose? How does she see you?"

He thought for a minute. "She sees me in my role as a Sunday school teacher and as a field trip parent. I usually say 'yes' to those things, and I enjoy doing them. But the rest . . . well, I just haven't been able to pull my life together in the way I thought I would, especially where work is concerned. And I've been in therapy before." He paused. "I'm not so sure it helped."

He had recently left an elementary school teaching position and was feeling at a loss about his career. This was not a new theme in his life. In his previous therapy, he had come to see a relationship between challenges he had faced as he was growing up and a pessimism he carried as an adult about finding meaningful and happy work. Yet, despite the therapy and his earnest longing to turn things around, the teaching had felt all wrong to him, and he was deeply discouraged about it.

"What do you see when you think about your growing-up years?" I asked him.

What he told was the story of a somber household, a little dreamlike. His father was vivid enough. He had been a stern and capricious enforcer in the family, chronically critical and sometimes rageful. But his mother and others in the extended family were more vague. "I don't know where my mother was," he said. "I can't find her when I think about our home in those days."

Over the next few sessions, a more positive story also appeared, though it was even more shadowy. As a young child, he would leave the house when his father was on a rampage and go over to the house of a neighbor who taught him woodworking in his basement shop. In school, he apprenticed himself to his science teachers and stayed as late after school as they would let him, working on special projects. These were descriptions of a resourceful young person, but he saw them only in glimpses, and he downplayed them with a sort of diffidence. "Yes, but . . ." he would say, if I pressed him for details.

Later, he became the only person in his family to go to college, and he traveled as far and wide as he could. Eventually, he set out for California with all his worldly possessions piled high on an ancient Volvo station wagon. He married happily and loved to spend time with his eight-year-old daughter. He was proficient at woodworking and photography, and enjoyed teaching Sunday school.

"Yes, but . . . ," he would say, and he would return to his discouragement about not getting his life together.

I told him about the Michael White weekend. "Suppose we pan back and witness these different stories that you tell yourself about yourself," I suggested.

"When you talk about 'the problem,' suppose we put those stories here." I swiveled my chair to the left and drew a place for them in the air. "And when you talk about your achievements, some you haven't even quite 'storied' yet," I said, swiveling to the right, "suppose we put those over here?"

There was bemusement in his face and then something a little lighter.

He and I got used to the idea that there were two sets of stories in the air. Maybe more. Definitely more.

We were back and forth among stories, in some great, good confusion. What happens if we locate ourselves *here?* Or *here?* Here is the teacher dropout, the one who can't get it together, the "product" of an abusive and neglectful family environment. Here is the person who came west in the old celery-green Volvo, the father who drives his daughter's forgotten lunch to school. Here's the person who slept poorly the other night, then is thrilled by a Jason Kidd no-look, under-the-basket pass and forgets he slept poorly.

We played around. We looked at the stories in the air.

But there was more still to come.

Quietly, irrevocably, something enormous has happened to Western man.

Huston Smith,
Beyond the Post-Modern Mind

METAPHYSICIAN HUSTON SMITH has written that the basic assumptions that underlie our understanding of the world are shifting radically, and that, "we of the current generation are playing a crucial but as yet not widely recognized part." The shift is too big, and we are too close. As scientists puzzle over what used to be called "matter," using equations that indicate probabilities or tendencies, psychotherapists puzzle over a person's life using language like "chosen meanings," "interpretive knowledge," and "candidate stories." Everybody is swimming in the postmodern soup.

Not so long ago, Adam Phillips, an English child psychoanalyst who looks closely at the stories people tell themselves, passed through Berkeley. Phillips has written that "people have traditionally come for psychoanalytic conversation because the story they are telling themselves about their lives has stopped, or become too painful, or both. The aim of the analysis is to restore the loose ends—and the looser beginnings—to the story."

Teased by that language, I attended his reading of a new paper, "Psychoanalysis and the Future of Fear," to a psychiatry grand-rounds audience of clinicians at a local hospital. It was a very dense paper, and it seemed to stun his audience. He looked up when he was finished reading and invited questions.

The room was dead quiet. If feet can be heard to shuffle on carpet, they were shuffling.

Finally, a hand went up. "Would you reread your last paragraph?" There was a little laughter.

Phillips sighed. "At least, you're just asking for the last paragraph," he said. "Last night, in San Francisco, I was asked to reread the whole paper."

Phillips' revolutionary query to himself and to his audience explodes through the tightness of his writing. What can we really know with any certainty about a person? he asks. "How can I learn who I am, when any belief I might come to about it assumes that life is not an open proposition?"

Phillips reread the last paragraph of his paper and looked out over the microphone again. The silence was uncomfortable. He and the grand-rounds audience, usually robust in its questioning of a presenter, regarded each other like mismatched socks.

Then a psychiatrist stood up.

"I'm seeing a young boy," he said sternly, "whose mother supports her crack cocaine habit with prostitution and whose father has been prevented from seeing them by court order because he was violent with them both. Sometimes the father kidnaps this boy and tortures him to learn about the mother's activities. Now, don't you think we know something about this child?"

At the podium, Phillips rested his face in his hand for a second. I imagined that he was suffering twice—suffering the boy's pain, and suffering the blunt confrontation of his colleague.

"If we think we know who this boy is," he said carefully, choosing his words, "then we are pretending that we know the future. And the past. And we don't."

The room was even quieter than before. Finally a therapist in the back raised her hand and called up, "You seem to tolerate ambiguity."

"Is that how I come across?" Phillips grinned now, and the tension in the room eased a little. "Actually, I enjoy ambiguity. It's interesting to consider why there is more than one person in the world. Whenever there is more than one, there are perspectives on a thing."

I want to say the truth which I don't know.
Nikita Mikhalkov,
director of *Burnt by the Sun*

IT'S NOT THAT NEWTON was wrong . . . exactly. Or Freud. Or the psychiatrist who earnestly believes that he knows his young patient. Newton's descriptions of what science now calls "large objects" were accurate and useful. They were only "wrong" once he edited out the rest of his philosophy of nature, which spoke of a vibrant universe infused with a creative principle. They were "wrong" in the sense that they were *partial* descriptions that came to be taken for descriptions of the whole. And once Freud's notion of "soul" was lost in mistranslation, he became identified with the objective study of a person's psychological world, analogous to the objective study of Newton's large-object world.

Through the ages, theories have been launched like flares, testifying to our deep yearning to understand the universe and our place in it. But in the end, theories are helpless to describe more than the "piece" of "reality" they momentarily illuminate.

They are necessarily personal and local descriptions. The water looks like this to me now, my mother's snapshot says, but the moment will quickly pass, and it will look like something else. The diarist Anaïs Nin wrote, "We see the world not as it is but as we are." Postmodern scientists go further and say the world *is* not as it is but as we are in it. The postmodern recognition that there are multiple views—and that every view is valid—reinstates our perceptions as legitimate and true, and so, in the midst of living, we are back in the universe again.

Toward the end of that October weekend in Napa Valley, I mentioned to Michael White, during a break, that he seemed to be allergic to hierarchy.

He seemed startled. Too personal maybe, I thought.

"Thank you for noticing!" he said then. He said it ringingly. "That is probably more true of me than anything else."

When Michael White turns, surprised, and acknowledges that he is allergic to hierarchy, or when Adam Phillips confirms with a grin that he enjoys the ambiguity of multiple perspectives, we get a shivery realization that orthodoxies are out the window. In postmodern psychotherapy, as in postmodern science, we have moved onto new ground.

This is good news and bad news. The good news is: Imagining a person's life as a collage of stories challenges the notion that there are some specifications somewhere about what a person is supposed to be like. The bad news is: Many stories can be dizzying to the point of nausea—postmodern nausea. When my client and I look at the "candidate stories" in the air about who he is, we can get pretty woozy. When he says, "Yes, but . . ." he's not kidding. He might well ask, "Yes, but then what *is* the story of me? Who am I really?" And it just might be tempting to return to the comforts of a conviction, even if it's a belief about being in the world as a mistreated and disheartened person.

But hold on. Postmodernism is a story too. Because it is in the business of unpacking all views of reality and holding them up for question—including its own view—the postmodern story makes it possible for us to stand back and see a progression of stories about how we've been making sense of things through time. Maybe the sequence is evolutionary.

Then, as we come blinking through the deconstructions of modern science and psychotherapy, one of those moments may arrive—one of those moments that transcends all these stories, freezing us in our tracks—and we see that the postmodern view of reality, like the modern view it has so stunningly overthrown, is not the end of the line.

. . .

ONE MORNING MY CLIENT, whose stories have been filling the room, comes in for my earliest appointment, sleepy and yawning. "I'm not awake yet," he says.

Sometimes I call this the pajama appointment. "Okay with me," I say. "Stay sleepy. Let's see what happens."

He sits quietly, a little slumped in the chair. "I feel really strange," he says after a while. "Both very large and very small. I've felt this before . . . as a kid. I would lie on my bed and watch the corner of my room fade back into infinity."

Infinity, I'm thinking. Big!

"In those days I was scared," he says.

"What about now?" I ask him.

"No, not really. This feels . . . this feels more like *possibility*."

Quiet.

"I can stay with it here, because it's a protected place." He says this almost distractedly, as if he were looking deep into this infinity.

"Did you tell anybody about these experiences when you were a child?" I say, after some time has gone by.

"No, no one to tell."

"Because . . . ?"

"Mostly, they were just too busy."

"If you could have told . . . ?"

"My life would have been completely different." He looks at me pointedly, then slides out into the deep place again.

"Different how?" I say after a while, hoping I'm not interrupting.

"I don't know what this is," he says, straightening himself up, "but it is *mine*. It is *me*. In my life I came to think something else was me. My activities were constantly criticized, so I spent my time trying to anticipate what would please people or at least keep me out of trouble. I was too busy to notice these moments of *me*."

"What led to your training to become a teacher?" Out of the blue, and not.

"*This*," he says. "But it didn't pan out in the school where I was. Others could . . . but I couldn't. It was pandemonium there, noisy all the time. These moments need quiet."

"Is helping children have their 'me' moments—in a way you couldn't—something you were wanting?"

"Yes. Absolutely."

Quiet.

"Finally," he says, stretching out in his chair. "Finally, this is me."

BUT CAN YOU

SEE IT?

the walk liberating, I was released from forms,
from the perpendiculars,
straight lines, blocks, boxes, binds
of thought
into the hues, shadings, rises, flowing bends and blends
of sight

A. R. AMMONS,
FROM "CORSON'S INLET"

THERE'S A STORY I sometimes tell, and I back it up with
a book of stereograms that I have lying around in my
office.

I was introduced to stereograms by my nephew during a
visit to my brother and sister-in-law's house in Southern California. Mathew was nine at the time. A big poster was tacked
to his bedroom door.

"Cool," I said. It was an intricate, psychedelic design in
specks of Day-Glo colors.

"But can you see it?" Mathew said.

"What do you mean 'it'?" I asked him. He was looking hard at my eyes, to see if he could tell. I was looking hard at his eyes to see what kind of trap this was.

"There's something there," he insisted. "Can you see it?"

"What?"

"Stand really close to it, and then back up slow. Look deep. Try to get in."

Get in? I stepped in close to the poster, to just a nose-length away and backed up slowly, crossing and uncrossing my eyes. What was I looking for? Then, just as I was deciding I'd been had by this beautiful child with the innocent face . . . just as I was starting to look back at him . . . something in the design shimmied. Deepened. With the sensation of elevator-stomach, I found that my eyes were dropping into it—into a dimension I had not suspected—and there I encountered a gigantic, leering Tyrannosaurus Rex, exploding up out of a lush tangle of jungle.

"Wow!" I breathed, involuntarily leaning back.

"You see it?"

"I see it!"

The poster on Mathew's door was a secret Jurassic world. He stood by quietly as I studied it, feeling the muscles of my eyes pull to accommodate the new depth.

"There's a pterodactyl flying out over the mountain! And a herd of those things that can run faster than a car!" Like I'm telling *him.*

"I know!" he said. "Isn't it cool?"

THIS STORY IS EMBLEMATIC for me of the moments in psychotherapy when the familiar pattern shimmies or shifts and a person drops into a hidden dimension with an exclamation of surprise.

About the time that Mathew was introducing me to stereograms in the San Diego mountains, two tectonic plates shifted a hundred miles to the north, near Los Angeles, and the area was rocked by a violent earthquake. The exclamation of a woman whose home was at the epicenter of the quake appeared in the newspaper the next morning. "I was looking at the ceiling," she said in perfect adrenaline shorthand, "and then I saw the sky." It's that kind of surprise.

The woman's words were so evocative for the composer Peter Sellars that a couple of years later he used them for the title of his new opera. Of course, earthquakes are more problematic than stereograms, if we are to take them as metaphors for revelation. Lives were lost in the Northridge earthquake, and damage was estimated in the billions of dollars. Yet revelation, transcendent and transforming, *is* dangerous. It is an elevator-stomach moment, a stop everything. The twentieth century abounds in tales of such moments in all realms of exploration. One of my favorites is a story about Einstein.

"IT MAY NOT seem so," Einstein said, "but the patent office was a better place for me to work than the university."

He was speaking of the year 1905, his *annus mirabilis*. After applying unsuccessfully to a number of European universities, he had finally landed a job as a routine examiner in a Swiss patent office in Bern. He found he could do his work quickly there and have time left over to daydream. Pushing back from his functionaire's desk, he would gaze at the patterns of light and motion in the dust motes as they floated around him and puzzle about the relationship of objects to the speed of their movement.

On a walk one day, he was sharing some of these puzzlings with a physicist friend walking with him. He was missing something important about the relationship of matter and energy, he said, and in just that moment he saw it. Excusing himself, he ran all the way back to his desk to try some calculations. It was not that the speed of light was variable, as he and others had been thinking. It was that the flow of time itself is variable. All of "reality" is relative, he saw, depending on where one stands in relation to it. Time, or where one stands in time, becomes the fourth dimension of a person's experience and of the physical universe itself.

Mathew's stereogram comes to mind. It was as if Einstein had suddenly found his way into a deeper landscape that had been there all along.

Another story, strikingly similar, was told by the physicist Werner Heisenberg. He and Neils Bohr, puzzling over their research, would agonize late into the night about their inability to reconcile their findings with the principles of classical physics. "I repeated to myself again and again the question, 'Can nature be so absurd as it seems to us in these subatomic experiments?'" he reported later.

In the summer of 1925, Heisenberg, at the age of 24, took himself—sick with hay fever and commotion of the mind—

away to the hill country of Helgoland. There, like Einstein, he walked. Then, in a day and a night, it came to him. He saw that subatomic "building blocks" of matter cannot be said to have a definite location in place or time but exist in a different realm entirely—in the mysterious and changeable realm of tendencies and probabilities. This was the discovery that would be called quantum mechanics.

Yet another tale of a twentieth-century discovery that had its origins in a walk is told by Evelyn Fox Keller in her biography of the Nobel Prize–winning geneticist Barbara McClintock, which she meaningfully entitled, *A Feeling for the Organism.*

McClintock was a precocious student, and she was also, from the time of her early childhood, an adventurous explorer of the unorthodox—she ran in the style of the running lamas of Tibet, practiced Eastern meditation rituals, explored extrasensory perception, and experimented with the mental control of her own body's temperature and blood pressure. As a graduate student at Stanford University, she was struggling to understand the genetic patterns of a red bread mold called *Neurospora*. At that time, genetics was usually studied by breeding an organism and studying its progeny to learn which characteristics were passed from one generation to the next.

McClintock wondered whether she could shortcut this technique, which was time consuming and tedious, by looking directly at the chromosomes. But as she stared through her microscope hour after hour, she could not make sense of what she was looking at.

"I wasn't seeing things," she told Keller. "I was lost."

Discouraged, which was uncharacteristic of McClintock, she sensed there might be something wrong with the way she was looking. She got up from her microscope, thinking that she had to "do something" with herself, and went for a walk among the huge eucalyptus trees on the campus. After a while, she settled onto a bench and despaired that she had taken on a project that was too difficult. Then, she said, she dropped into "this very intense, subconscious thinking. And suddenly I knew everything was going to be just fine." She jumped up and ran back to the lab. Now, as she looked into her microscope, she found that everything had gotten *bigger*.

"I was right down there with them," she said, reminding me of the happy day I found I could swim around in my pond water village in Mr. Emery's class, "and these were my friends."

To McClintock's amazement, genes were moving along the chromosome strand, and sometimes even jumping from one chromosome to another. What could be tripping off all this activity? Eventually, she was able to show that information was flowing not only from the genes, but also *to* the genes from the organism's environment in a complex two-way informational system. Seeing things no one had seen before, she found herself witness to an instantaneous and elegant mechanism for a "smart" and purposeful system of evolution that even Darwin had not suspected.

Einstein and McClintock were radicalized by their scientific epiphanies. For the rest of his life, Einstein was asked how he saw what he saw that day. "By wondering as a child wonders," he would answer. He was persuaded that the way to discovery was intuitive, not logical. More than that, it was personal and religious. "Cosmic religiosity," he called it.

McClintock put the question of how you know what you know a little differently. "*Why* do you know?" she asked. "Why were you so sure of something when you couldn't tell anyone else? You weren't sure in what I would call a boastful way; you were sure in what I call a completely internal way." What we call scientific knowledge is "lots of fun," she said to Keller. "You get correlations, but you don't get the truth. Things are much more marvelous than the scientific method allows us to conceive."

Ideas like these made McClintock controversial in the scientific community, and her Nobel Prize came late in her career. One time, after visiting her lab, the Nobel prize–winning physiologist Joshua Lederberg exclaimed, "By God, that woman is either crazy or a genius!" You learn about a thing, she believed, by opening yourself wholeheartedly to it. You learn about a thing by loving it.

· · ·

AFTER SUFFERING A cerebral hemorrhage during a stage performance with her bluegrass band, a young mother of two small children comes to her appointments in a motorized wheelchair. It's been a couple of years now. The stroke has turned her life upside down. The right side of her body is unresponsive, her professional life is on hold, and she is not able to take care of her children without help. Her husband has recently separated from her and is living with another woman.

Words come slowly for this woman now, and when she speaks her meanings are dense, like haiku.

"I'm jealous," she said one morning.

I was relieved that it was coming up. We had been talking about practical things, but she had not said very much about the huge upheavals in her family and the heartbreaks.

"But it's not what you think," she said, stopping me short. "I'm jealous of myself. Before the stroke."

I was stunned by this. I had been going down a wrong road.

She sat quietly for a minute and then began to talk about her life before and after the stroke. With an economy of words, she spoke about how much she has lost and how much harder it is for her to do everything now.

After a while, she paused, tired.

I was struck by the starkness of it, and by the beauty of her telling. I could only tell her that I found her ability to deliver a big message in a few words poetic.

She took my compliment with a wry smile. We had discovered some time back that we had done our undergraduate work at the same college and had studied William Blake with the same professor.

"There's a story about Stephen Hawking," I said.

She nodded. She knows about Hawking, the British cosmologist who suffers from a motor neuron affliction called amyotrophic lateral sclerosis (ALS), or Lou Gehrig's disease. And she understands what ALS has done to his body.

"As his ALS progressed and he began to lose his ability to speak," I told her, "he noticed that his thinking—which had tended to conform to linear language, as thinking does— began to open out. His mind's eye, I guess, began to 'see' more spacially, and he experienced a leap in his ability to imagine multidimensional models of the universe."

I had often tried to imagine what a multidimensional universe might look like.

"Have you noticed anything like that?" I asked her. "Is there anything different about your before-stroke and after-stroke thoughts? Anything that runs through both?"

She thought for a long time. I wondered if she had moved on to something else. Then the tiredness in her eyes softened, and a richness of expression began to shine through the partial paralysis of her face.

"No," she said slowly. "But I just discovered something. You know the before-stroke and after-stroke 'me?' *I* . . . am in both. Untouched."

Her vocal chords have been affected by her stroke, so her range of voice tones has been diminished. It makes it hard for her to lend emphasis to her words. So she said it again, "Untouched."

Then she smiled a marvelous, crooked smile.

> *Take a moment to consider this. Look at your hand. Now look at the light streaming from the lamp beside you. And at the dog resting at your feet. You are not merely made of the same things. You are the same thing. One thing. Unbroken.*
>
> Michael Talbot,
> *The Holographic Universe*

A FEW DAYS AFTER this session, it happened that Stephen Hawking came to town. In honor of Hawking's visit, a panel made up of a cosmologist, a mathematician, a philosopher of science, and a theologian met on the stage of Zellerbach Hall at the University of California, Berkeley, for a public conversation about whether science amounts to an *unveiling* or an *invention* of reality.

In his opening remarks, Roger Penrose, the British mathematician and pioneer of black hole theory, seemed to come down on the side of science as an unveiling. He said that while there is an extraordinary accuracy in our ability to describe nature—quantum electrodynamics, for example, can measure the distance between New York and Los Angeles to "within a half-breadth of a hair"—the real advances in mathematics feel more to him like discoveries, not simply computations.

As the conversation continued, I sat there among young students in the audience, marveling at the difference between the questions that were going back and forth among the panelists—questions about God, social context, the nature of reality—and my old high school physics class, dry-as-ever-loving-dust, about levers and ergs. Here was the Australian cosmologist Paul Davies, an out-of-the-closet believer in science as a more reliable pathway to God than religion, chiding scientists, especially North Atlantic scientists, about their compulsive secularism.

Then, from somewhere near the back of the auditorium, a student shouted up a question for Roger Penrose. "Are you equating mathematics with God?" he asked.

Penrose was quick and emphatic in his response. "No!" he shouted a little unnecessarily into his microphone. Then he paused, studying something in front of him on the speakers' table. "No," he said again more quietly, "but . . . I'm beginning to glimpse something . . . something . . . that is beyond the rules of computation but is still *comprehensible*. I can't speak of it yet—can't conceive it yet."

It seemed to me that a hush fell over the auditorium, as if we were all looking with him.

I walked home from campus that night, scanning the winter constellations as I went along. I thought of the awful night skies at Silver Bay and my difficulty telling anyone about those nighttime questions I turned over and over like rough stones: *Who am I? Where is all of this coming from?* And I marveled that a cosmologist haltingly tells a university audience, in response to a question about God, that he is getting glimpses of an underlying something, comprehensible somehow in a realm beyond computation.

The next night, Stephen Hawking spoke to a sold-out, standing-room-only crowd at Berkeley Community Theater. Hawking was born exactly three hundred years after the death of Galileo, and he holds the Lucasian Chair of Physics at Cambridge University, the chair once held by Isaac Newton. Up on the stage, he was a tiny figure in a fancy wheelchair with attached keyboard, his body crumpled by ALS. A large video screen helped those of us in the back see his face.

There was something riveting about Hawking's "voice," electronically constructed from his keyboard, and his droll humor as he led us through his frontier ideas about "stable chaos," the birth of the universe, and the astonishing math behind the idea that the stuff of the universe has a very particular "critical density" that holds us in a delicate balance between an infinite expansion, the Big Bang, and an infinite contraction, the Big Crunch.

Hawking predicted that by the time the sun blows up, we should have mastered interstellar travel, provided that we haven't destroyed ourselves first. But, he warned, navigating through black holes could be too fast—we might turn into spaghetti. "The best evidence that we haven't yet discovered time travel," he said, twinkling all the way to the back row, "is that we haven't been invaded by the future."

At the end of his talk, Hawking seemed tired. He was wheeled off stage to rest and would come back again, we were told, to answer a few questions. We were invited to write our questions on scraps of paper and pass them to the aisles. Everyone in the auditorium seemed to be writing, and pretty soon the baskets of collected questions were piled high. Backstage, Hawking must have read fast, while we in the audience buzzed like Cinderella's sisters about whose questions he would choose. When he returned, he had chosen two.

He read the first question: "'Do you believe in God?' I am asked this question often," he said, looking out at us. "Like Einstein, I do not believe in a personal God. But one has to ask the question, Why does the universe bother to exist? If you like, you can make God the answer to that question."

The second question. "'What would you say to the population of disabled people in Berkeley?'" he read. There were many wheelchairs in the audience. "Disabled people must concentrate on areas in which they can compete with anyone," he said in the curious electronic voice. Then he added, "I don't want to be known as a great, disabled scientist. I want to be known as a great scientist."

THE NEXT WEEKEND, I settled into a more or less body-shaped place on the jagged headlands of the Mendocino coast as a heavy green surf thundered in, shaking the coastline and sending up slow-motion spray. Overhead the sun was trying to burn through a thinning film of fog. On my rock, I was thinking about my client. I would have to tell her about my latest brush with Stephen Hawking—how he had chosen, from a bushel basket full of questions, one about God, and one that gave him a way to share with the audience what he believes and doesn't believe about the limitations of physical disability.

When my client discovers a wholly intact *I* that runs through the before-stroke and after-stroke circumstances of her body, her suffering yields, and she takes her place among the most serious investigators of—as Stephen Hawking frames it—how the universe works and why we are here.

How shall we understand what has happened? What has opened the way?

There is something deep, something elusive still missing in our understanding of how the world works. What is certain is that a person can slip into an alignment with these workings. Often while walking out under the sky. Indoors or out. On legs or in wheelchairs. There, on a lucky day, we see something.

IF YOU CAN'T MEDITATE,

TRAVEL

*The answer to how the pigeon finds its way home
is that a portion of the pigeon's mind is already home,
and never left home.*

TERENCE MCKENNA,
THE EVOLUTIONARY MIND

REMEMBER WHEN I discovered exactly who I was and where I was going?" he said, looking bleak. I was talking with my biochemist-gymnast client who, sometime earlier, had discovered fairies.

He'd come back to therapy, suffering now from debilitating pain and weakness radiating down from his neck into his arms and hands. His symptoms were thought to be a new repetitive-activity syndrome caused by long hours at his computer keyboard, an inevitable part of his research work. As a consequence, he'd been banished from the keyboard and was in his third month of medical leave from the lab. Bored senseless and discouraged, he had recently switched to a new neurologist, who had taken him off all anti-inflammatory medications and prescribed rest and physical therapy.

"This approach feels more right," he said. "Those meds were getting me nowhere, but my progress is so slow. It's weird—I look fine, but I can't do anything. Nobody gets it." He described lying around alone in his apartment—he was not supposed to sit—dozing off into a limbo state, and then waking up startled and disoriented.

"It's said they used to punish inmates on Alcatraz by not letting them work," I told him. "This is hard duty."

"Well, I have sneaked in a little work on this." He handed me an updated draft of his curriculum vitae. "If my sit-down days at the computer are over, I need to figure out what's next. I've tried slanting my CV toward teaching."

I scanned down the pages. They detailed his rich education and training experience.

"What's this award?" I asked him. I had just gotten to the section that listed his outside interests and activities. It included an award for the "Most Inspirational Gymnast." This was not something I knew about.

He was surprised. "I never told you about that?" he said.

"Don't think so," I said.

"My car accident?"

I shook my head.

"After my car accident . . ." he started, and looked down. "The surgeon who put the rod in my leg said I would never do gymnastics again. I remember thinking, 'Just watch me.' But I also remember thinking, 'What if it's true?'"

"And . . . ?" I was impatient to hear more.

"Are you sure I haven't . . . ?"

"Positive."

"Well, it was my goal to walk without a limp. I spent a lot of time in the weight room. I think I looked like a pretty sorry, depressed son of a bitch. Really bitter. I had all these fantasies about what I'd like to do to the leg of the driver who hit me. . . . But then I started to work out with my friend, Curt. I was weak, and I got tired easily, but I noticed that Curt would get tired, too. I started to feel something like, 'It's still there.' I decided I would come back. And then I was competing again in a few months."

I sat there shaking my head over the stories we forget to tell each other, forget to tell ourselves.

He went on, choosing his words. "You know how people talk about the innate human spirit? I was experiencing it myself. I was experiencing it *in* myself. I was still surprised about the Most Inspirational Gymnast award, though. I didn't know anybody was paying that much attention."

We both sat quietly for a minute, just taking all this in.

He spread his hands and studied them. "I haven't thought about that injury for a long time." He paused. "I had a 'For what?' back then."

"A 'For what?'"

"A 'What is this for?' And I knew. With the injury, I had a challenge, a clear sense of purpose. I wanted to come back. And that's when I discovered the innate-spirit part. But with this injury, I haven't had the 'For what?' All the warnings I've had to watch out, not make it worse, all the lying around . . . I just haven't found the same sense of purpose."

In these last few minutes, I had been seeing him, in my mind's eye, walking down at the waterfront park that looks out over San Francisco Bay and, beyond the Golden Gate Bridge, the forever of the Pacific Ocean. "Can you walk two miles?"

"Probably. I haven't, but I probably could."

"Have you ever walked the loop at the marina? Level, about two miles. There's a lot of water, a lot of sky."

"Huh. I've never been there."

"What about walking with the question, 'For what?' without making any effort at finding an answer. Just offering up the question as you walk."

"Fairies, you think?" he said.

Something there is that doesn't love a wall,
That wants it down.

Robert Frost,
from "Mending Wall"

THERE'S A JOKE in the American Buddhist community that goes, "If you can't meditate, travel." The instruction is obvious: Do whatever it takes to bust out. The joke, though not many people on the street would say so, could be about fractals.

"Fractal" is another new word on the scene—like "deconstruction" or quantum "mechanics"—that means the opposite of what you think it's going to mean. It sounds like something hard, or hard-edged. Maybe it's a piece of something that broke when it was dropped. But no, a fractal is the opposite of hard. It's like the diaphanous edges of a cloud. It *is* the diaphanous edges of a cloud.

In the 1960s, the quantum pioneer Werner Heisenberg warned his readers, in effect, about the hazards of nondiaphanous edges. In *Physics and Philosophy,* he said that the hard partition between mind and matter, installed in Western cosmology in the course of the Scientific Age, would make it extremely difficult for twentieth-century quantum theorists to interpret their own mystifying findings. "This partition," he wrote, "has penetrated deeply into the human mind during the three centuries following Descartes, and it will take a long time for it to be replaced by a really different attitude toward the problem of reality."

Fractals are partitions gone indistinct. I learned about them in a terrific book with the terrific title, *The Evolutionary Mind: Trialogues at the Edge of the Unthinkable.* The book is a transcription of the conversations of the biologist Rupert Sheldrake, shamanologist Terence McKenna, and mathematician and chaos scientist Ralph Abraham. These friends are talking about everything under the sun—science, psychedelics, psychic animals, the World Wide Web.

A fractal, in strict geometric terms, is an iterative formula that feeds its answers to itself and recomputes. This definition is more than daunting to me, but Abraham uses familiar images in nature to demystify fractals. Imagine, he says, that you are looking at the shoreline of Hawaii on a map. Here's the land, here's the blue sea, separated by a hard edge. But when we walk along the sandy beach we see—we feel underfoot— that this edge is more like a transition: There is water in the sand and sand in the water. "The Milky Way," he says, "is a sandy beach in the sky." Fractals are about something shading into something else; they are about motion. They are about infinity.

Abraham teaches that boundaries that are too firm or too rigid are like iron curtains. They are not porous enough or crooked enough—it's hard to find just the right word—for living systems to thrive. A cell, a person, a relationship, an international political process—systems at all of these levels have to have enough chaos.

Enough chaos?

Abraham is not talking here about chaos in the sense of murder and mayhem. He is using the word chaos more like the ancient Greeks used it, like Newton used it—an infinity of energy or formless matter that preceded and gave rise to the ordered universe. It was in this sense that Abaham and other mathematicians in the 1980s spoke of an underlying order in the seemingly random, turbulent phenomena in nature. Now chaos theory has burgeoned into an explosive new field of inquiry that takes its place, some say, with relativity and quantum mechanics as one of the three most important advances of twentieth-century science.

All things spring from chaos, Aristotle said. Newton said it too. It is the process of this springing, this becoming—and the vast, mysterious matrix that it *becomes-from*—that so intrigues chaos theorists. They watch patterns of smoke wafting, water dripping, a person thinking, and they watch how rigid partitions get in the way.

A naturally flowing stream of water will always try to create a meandering course. In a broad valley, a river will swing in wide, graceful loops; in a narrow valley, it will flow in a tighter, winding pattern. Least at home in the artificial banks of an irrigation canal or a levy system, a stream will eat away at its constraints, trying to break out. In the same way, an electron—if it could be captured inside walls that begin to close in on it—moves faster and faster, banging off the walls as if it were frantically claustrophobic. When elements in nature, like water or electrons, bump up against boundaries that are too rigid or tight for them to move in their natural patterns of space and motion, they might be said to be suffering a poverty of chaos.

People too. People come for psychotherapy because something about their lives—a belief or a way of experiencing the world—has become too tight. We saw that Adam Phillips talks about the therapeutic conversation as a project aimed at restoring "the loose ends—and the looser beginnings—to the story." Ralph Abraham talks about fractals as "frothy zones."

Suppose, he says, "the psychotherapist is trained in chaos theory instead of Freudian theory." When an intrapsychic boundary is not fractal enough, a therapy would be devised to increase its fractal dimension, making it more porous so that the universe can flow through more freely.

My client's "For what?" question (with apologies to Abraham) "fractalizes" him, softening something that has been holding him tight, too tight, even as he has struggled to find just the right doctor and comply with just the right treatment strategy. It softens the belief he has labored under before, that he is broken or broken-off-from. With the idea that there might be something else out there—something he has already found—he breaks out. Back out in the universe again, he remembers the intimations he has had of "the bigger place." He remembers his fairies.

YOU DON'T HAVE TO BE housebound with physical pain to suffer from a poverty of chaos. You can be inside a skintight skin in all kinds of ways. You can be culture bound, theory bound, belief bound.

You can be fear bound.

A couple of years ago, John and I made a trip to Southeast Asia. To me, it seemed as far away as the moon, and I was anxious about absolutely everything—unexploded land mines, teenagers packing around AK-47s, malaria, everything.

While we were in Cambodia, we were invited to visit a small teaching hospital in Phnom Penh, built by Westerners with Western funding to train Cambodian medical students and treat the poorest of Cambodia's post-war poor. The hospital's public relations director, an Australian expatriate, suggested that the best time for a tour was early, before the day got too hot. She and her driver, a Cambodian first-year medical student, picked us up at our hotel at seven o'clock sharp. As we bumped along Phnom Penh's dusty, potholed streets, she turned to visit with us in the backseat. The hospital, she said, gesturing out the window, was located in a tough, run-down part of town.

All of Phnom Penh looks run-down. It looks like it has been through hell—which it has. So I was a little surprised by her apology, if that's what it was. But mostly, I was just trying to be ready for whatever we were about to see.

As we made our way into the makeshift parking lot a few minutes later and parked among a tangle of bikes and moto-bikes, I could see that some three hundred patients and their families had already gathered in front of the hospital, and more were coming. They had been traveling, many on foot, from all corners of Cambodia. People of all ages, some terribly thin, were sitting or lying quietly on rows of backless wooden benches under a corrugated awning, waiting to be triaged at folding tables just outside the front door of the building. Some turned to watch us as we walked up, shading their eyes in the early-morning sun.

Caught somewhere between trying to see and trying not to, I scanned this scene as if I were looking through my fingers at a terrifying movie. I was looking for something I could use as a visual mantra to steady myself—a green tree maybe, or the flash of a bird. But there are no birds in Cambodia. They have all been eaten by people struggling to survive. And there is precious little green.

John was scanning, too, but differently. He recognized this early morning line-up from his year, before the war, as a bush doctor in a jungle village called Kratie, on the Mekong River. He was scanning, as he would have scanned the morning crowd in front of his own medical station, for malaria, tuber-culosis, malnutrition, traumatic injuries.

We both noticed a woman in a wheelchair at the same time. She was near the front of the line.

"Leprosy," John said quietly. "Early. You can't see it in her face or her fingers yet, but those white blotches on her arms—if you poked one with a needle she wouldn't be able to feel it."

Wheelchairs are in short supply in Cambodia. Maybe that was why we spotted her first. She sat looking grateful for her chair, looking dreamy even, as two younger women were attending her, massaging her shoulders and upper arms almost absentmindedly, with hands that seemed to know what they were doing. All three wore dark *sarongs* and brightly-colored *kramas,* which wound gracefully around their shoulders and heads.

"Is she in pain?" I asked John. But, strangely, as I heard the echo of my own question, it was as if it had come from a place I had already left. Looking at this landscape of unimaginable horror through the fingers of my own fear, I realized that this woman in the wheelchair had become my mantra.

"Probably not. More likely numbness . . ." John was saying, but I wasn't really listening.

I was settling down now, unclenching, and I found that I could look, really look, into her face as she was looking into mine. The world that had been buzzing all around with quiet conversations went silent for a minute.

I could see her now. She was calm and undismayed by whatever was going on in her body, and she was curious about me. With a sudden sob in my throat, I could see that she was perfectly all right, and so was I—two windows on a world of perfect all-right-ness.

I must have jumped when our public relations guide urged us toward the front doors for our promised tour of the lab, surgery, and small inpatient ward. "We see a lot of that," she was saying as she led us through another crowd of people waiting just inside. She must have noticed that my attention had been captured by the patient with leprosy and the women who were with her. "Family members often seem to express their anxiety in that fretful way," she said, "rubbing and rubbing the person who is sick."

A COUPLE OF DAYS LATER, I asked a friend, an American expatriate working in the south of Cambodia, if she knew anything about traditional Cambodian massage. I told her about the massage we had seen in front of the hospital in Phnom Penh and said that it had looked to me like acupressure, with attention to certain points across the shoulders and down the arms.

"I don't know anything about acupressure points," she said, "but, wait a minute . . ." She bent over to roll up her pant leg, exposing a line that ran up the side of her leg. "One time I sliced my leg open on the bumper of a car when the moto I was riding passed too close. See, I still have the scar."

It was an impressive scar, long, but nicely mended.

"I was out in the country," she went on, "and the only medical facility was a storefront clinic that had sutures but no anesthesia. The nurse had me lie down on a table, and then she called over a couple of women who were passing by. They massaged my leg as she sewed me up, and I remember being surprised that there was almost no pain. Tugging, but no pain. It's funny—I'd forgotten all about this—I hate needles, but I remember feeling very calm."

She thought for a moment. "It could be, I guess. I never thought about it. It might have had something to do with acupressure. "

HOME FROM CAMBODIA, I had long talks with myself about how we know what we know and about how tight the compartments can become. I thought how easy it would be to mistake a purposeful massage, backed up by centuries of a different kind of knowing, for something casual, or something fretful. And I thought about the long look that had passed between me and the woman in the wheelchair.

We know the world is bigger than our minds can comprehend. And then sometimes the mind can be surprised out of its own compartments, and in the moment of surprise, we see—we remember—that there is more, much more.

Look on the periphery of the image.
What do you see?

Dick Olney

IF YOU CAN'T meditate *or* travel, get to a weekend workshop with Dick Olney.

Dick has died now, but he is very much in the hearts of those of us who worked with him and loved him. For years, practitioners of one kind or another—people hoping to break through to something new—would gather around whenever Dick came to town. At regular intervals, he would travel from his home in Milwaukee to Berkeley and to other places around the country to percolate his ideas about healing and wellness in workshops that he called "Self-Acceptance Training."

Remarkable things happened in those workshops. Many stories could be told in a chapter about fractals—a notion that would have intrigued him, I think—but the one that comes to mind is about a friend and colleague who broke out of a very tight and painful place. Or maybe it's truer to say that Dick broke her out.

Dick always began the day's work the same way. A big man with a broad, generous face and big hands, he sat, a little stooped, drumming on a very deep drum. Sometimes he added the sound of his very deep voice, chanting and improvising with the drum, and then others would join in with their drums and rattles and song. The sound would build and build, and soon the room opened, or deepened, to a palpable resonance that seemed to say, "What you have come looking for is here. And everywhere. And always was."

People would take turns working with Dick, one-on-one, while the rest of the group sat around in a loose circle, watching quietly. One afternoon, a friend of mine decided to take a turn. As she and Dick sat facing each other cross-legged on the floor, she told about her difficult relationship with her father—about how exacting and critical he was, and how hard it had always been to win his appreciation for her considerable academic and professional achievements. As an expert consultant she had even been on *Oprah!* A few tears squeezed out now from behind her tightly closed eyelids. Life always seemed like a test she was failing, she said, and her work—"like a prophecy fulfilled"—was feeling flat.

Dick spoke up now. He asked her to notice that she was referring to her history in the present tense.

"You say, 'I can't feel good about my work,' as if you see yourself as an unchanging object. Try saying, 'I haven't been able to feel good about my work,' and let's see what happens. It's a more accurate statement, and it's more open-ended. It implies that you are a *process* that can conceivably change at any moment, which is the truth."

She thought this over. She adored Dick, and she trusted him, but when she took up the story again, with eyes still closed, she was still in the present tense. It was as if she were a captive of her own syntax, in some permanent, now-and-forever trap.

After a while, Dick—never one to get up off the floor easily—lumbered to his feet. He picked his way awkwardly through the group, joints cracking and popping, and went into an adjoining room of the house. In a minute he reappeared, holding something in his big hands. My friend was still talking, still tearful; she had not missed him.

Dick sat down again with more cracking and popping and painstakingly spread an array of brilliant yellow gingko leaves he had collected on his early morning walk. Then he waited.

The leaves lay in a pool in front of her, radiating their color onto her face, which glowed now with a do-you-like-butter reflection of yellow. She was still talking. Dick waited quietly. Some people in the group chuckled softly. Still talking.

Finally, Dick said. "Open your eyes and look!" He said it with real authority.

For a minute, it seemed too hard for her to do. At last she opened her eyes, but now she stared at the leaves without seeing them. Nobody made a sound. Finally, after a long moment, her breathing changed.

"Oh my God," she said quietly.

"Exactly!" Dick said.

Now her tears were different, lush, and her face was soft and open. She picked up one of the fan-shaped leaves and gazed at it for a long time, rubbing the ribby texture between her thumb and forefinger.

"Would you like sharing?" Dick asked her, as he always did at the end of a piece of work. She nodded, looking around at us as if we had just arrived.

"Is there sharing?" he asked.

At first we all just breathed out in one big exhalation. Then one person after another thanked her for her work. Some spoke of their struggles in coming to terms with similar messages from their parents, and all around there were murmurs of familiarity and appreciation.

DICK NEVER WROTE a book about his work, but he sometimes spoke of Aldous Huxley's *The Perennial Philosophy*. Huxley had been looking for a common factor in all philosophical and religious explorations of what he called the "immemorial and universal" in human experience.

Dick, who had never trained as a psychologist, had been looking for the common factor in "a perennial therapy" and had come to believe that the prevailing theme of his work was a certain tone or resonance he came to call "self-acceptance." He was not talking about self-acceptance in the sense of self-approval or resigned disapproval, but in the sense of an unhindered self in a full and openhearted relationship with itself and with the world. For Dick, this amounted to the discovery of "who I really am."

It's what we call the "identity" or "personality" or "self-image"—the who-I-*think*-I-am-or-ought-to-be—that gets in the way of the who-I-*really*-am, Dick said. But as much as we might like to change or suspend this problematic self-image, "you can't change the self-image head-on with the conscious mind," he would say, waggling his finger in the vicinity of a person's head, "not until hell freezes over." You have to be cagey and watch to see what comes in from the edges.

When Dick talked like this, I always thought of the particular kind of tunnel blindness that is caused by macular degeneration. You can't see anything in the middle of your field of vision; you can only see what's out on the periphery. You can't see yourself straight-on in the mirror, Dick was saying. You have to deduce something about yourself from the edges.

But with this new idea about fractals—at least the way Ralph Abraham is talking about them—I wonder.

Abraham says, "It takes only very subtle medicine to decrease rigid walls. Even the very idea of it may be enough. After all, nature is playing a part."

My gymnast-scientist client stops me cold when he reports that he is getting straight-on intimations of a "bigger place." "It's bigger," he says, "much bigger. I don't see any edges to it." His noticing is the medicine. And his ability to notice his noticing, and to tell about it, sends me into some hard wondering about our contemplations of human consciousness. Is the boundary between what we have been calling the "conscious" and the "unconscious" more "frothy" than we have been imagining? Was Dick really right? Is it true that the distortions and dilemmas posed by a person's "self-image"—the too-tightness—cannot be taken head-on, not until hell freezes over?

· · ·

JUGGLING THESE QUESTIONS about conscious and unconscious knowing—and how separate they are or aren't from each other—I think about another experience that John and I brought home from our trip to Southeast Asia.

The person John most wanted to see in Cambodia was Sun Leng, the widow of a close friend who had been executed, along with many others, on the first day of Pol Pot's brutal takeover of the country. John had known Sun Leng and her husband before the war. He knew she had somehow survived, though her health was failing now. We were directed to her village in the south of the country by her daughter, Monie, who happened by chance to be in Phnom Penh while we were there.

"You must see my mother!" Monie had said. "She has much to tell you."

We were already planning a car trip to a nearby village in the south to visit our expatriate friend, and we told Monie we would try to find Sun Leng from there. John was more and more eager to see her, and his knowledge of the Khmer language had come back well enough that he would be able to talk to her without a translator. But everything in Cambodia is difficult. We found that the road between the village we were visiting and Sun Leng's village had been bombed out in the war and was impassable even by moto. There was no way to get to her, and we were running out of time. We bumped our way back to Phnom Penh on a road that was bad enough, tired, frustrated, and deeply disappointed.

We'd only been back in our hotel room a few minutes when the phone rang. It was Monie.

"Guess who's here?"

"Where?" John shouted. "Where?"

"We're in the lobby of your hotel."

John ran, and I watched as Sun Leng, a tiny woman of only eighty pounds, disappeared into his big embrace.

"How . . . ?" John stammered, after their first exchange of greetings in Khmer.

She explained that she had come on a passable road by bus.

"But how did you know?"

"That's what I asked her when she walked in the door!" Monie said. "I couldn't reach her, you couldn't reach her."

Sun Leng studied John's face for a minute. She said, "When I woke up this morning, I knew I had to come to Phnom Penh. I got on the bus. I didn't know why. "

"I told her why when she walked in," Monie said. "I told her, 'We have to catch a moto. John is in town!' Then she knew."

"A while ago I had a Chinese card reading," Sun Leng told John. "The reader said someone I care about very much was coming from a long distance. This morning I knew I needed to get on the bus."

JOHN AND I went to Southeast Asia with different agendas. He was on a personal healing mission. I was on a mission to explore my prejudice, or inverse prejudice, that the East understands those things so dear to my heart—nonlocal mind and spontaneous healing—better than we in the West do.

Besotted with a mix of physics envy and Eastern envy, I was the one who got a comeuppance.

The reunion of John and Sun Leng is a love story. It's the best story of our trip to Southeast Asia, and maybe it doesn't trivialize it too much to say that it invites us into big questions about where mind and matter dwell. How did Sun Leng know? How did the Chinese card reader?

But Sun Leng treated John's "How did you know?" offhandedly.

"I just knew," she said, waving off any fancy distinctions I might have wanted to make about "normal" and "paranormal" knowing, or any belief about which is the straightest road to heaven.

All this would have been enough to puzzle about, but there was more. There was the terrible pulsing of violence one feels in Cambodia under every footstep. Every person we met told of unimaginable brutality and loss they and their families have suffered. Their experiences are in their faces and in their carefully-chosen words. I reminded myself that these people had been mercilessly bombed by my own country, but then, they had killed each other by the millions in civil upheaval. My fascination with their preternatural—or maybe natural—knowing was eclipsed by my horror of the killing fields. How to reconcile clairvoyance with massacre and forced starvation? I put it to myself in a journal entry on the plane home.

"Here it is in a nutshell," I wrote. "There is a dimension of human experience here that is all but unknown in our 'Western' world. Southeast Asians do it, expect it, without thinking a thing about it. They hear each other across long distances. See things. Guess right. Anticipate. And yet they cut each other's throats with shovels. And, according to the friezes at Angkor Wat, they always have. I don't get it. Isn't it true that the better we know each other, the more empathy we have?"

Back home, I was deeply shaken. I called the metaphysician and religious scholar, Huston Smith, who happens to live just up the way. Huston has written about growing up in China with missionary parents. He has traveled the world with his wife, Kendra, who is a psychotherapist, and he has authored many important books, including the classic text *The World's Religions* and the more recent *Why Religion Matters*. He is equally comfortable talking about Eastern and Western religious philosophy. I asked him if he would look over my shoulder at what I had seen.

Come on over, he said most graciously.

Out on the Smiths' back porch, Huston listened attentively as I described the desperate poverty we had seen in Cambodia and Laos—so many beggars, so many amputees.

Then I told him the story of Sun Leng finding her way to us in Phnom Penh. He responded with a most improbable story of his own about how, in the milling masses of Shanghai, he had come upon the principal of the girls' school his parents had founded sixty years before in his boyhood town, seventy miles distant from where they were standing. We sat admiring each other's stories.

But, not usually one to shortchange marvelous tales, I needed to return to the violence I had felt, still palpable in Hun Sen's Cambodia. "It was like walking across the skin of a drum," I told him. "I can't reconcile the clairvoyance and the violence. I don't know how to explain any of this to myself."

He considered for a moment. "But do I detect an incipient hypothesis?"

"You mean, because I think people who can read each other like this ought to have a leg up on virtue?" I said.

"Yes," he said. "I think it may be a little romantic. The 'normal' and the 'paranormal'—the visible and the invisible—are just opposite sides of the same coin, different ways of human knowing. Neither is more highly evolved than the other."

His quiet words banged around in my head.

Then I began to see that synchronous experiences are part of a universe we don't understand, and so are epiphanies, but they are not the same. Sun Leng knew someone important to her was in Phnom Penh, and she knew it with such certainty that she got on the bus. This gift for knowing could, under different circumstances, be thought of as an exquisitely refined paranoia or vigilance, fear- or survival-based, born out of necessity. Such an experience can invite a person into contemplation of a universe more mysterious and marvelous than we had supposed—or not. An epiphany is the conscious recognition that the mind's edge has dissolved and a discovery is in the making. You see something about the world you had not seen before, and—with the help of fairies or gingko leaves—you see something about yourself.

"You know," I said finally, "Cambodia has ruined my mind."

"Congratulations!" Huston said. "Would you like some more tea?"

HELP ALREADY

ON THE WAY

And God said to the soul:
I desired you before the world began.
I desire you now
As you desire me.
And where the desires of two come together
There love is perfected.

MECHTHILDE OF MAGDEBURG,

FROM "GOD SPEAKS TO THE SOUL"

PEOPLE HAVE GONE to all kinds of trouble to alter ordinary, languaged states of mind in the hope of opening out into nonordinary states of consciousness. Aldous Huxley, in *Doors of Perception,* was careful to suggest that epiphanies—what he called "divine disclosures"—cannot be "caused," but they can sometimes be "occasioned" by confounding the mind. Stories from all corners of the world have told of shifts in perception experienced through accidental or intentional exposure to sacred art, sacred ritual, entheogenic drugs, feverish illness, exhaustion, ordeals in nature, the gnawing on a Zen koan.

A homelier strategy for the fractalizing of the mind, and one conspicuously less strenuous, is the use of prayer. I'm not (necessarily) speaking of the rote saying of a prayer or of beseeching God to intervene, as if He is falling down on the job and needs a gentle or not-so-gentle nudge. An open-ended "Thy will be done," as we have seen in an earlier chapter seems to work just fine—however a person thinks of "Thy."

From time immemorial, people have known that prayer helps us access the ineffable, and even more practically, that prayer helps us heal.

Think of this for a moment: Prayer heals! This irreducible fact—and the recognition that something primal about the universe is revealed in the process—is more than a mystery to us. Taking it slowly, it means that changes in the human mind "occasion," to use Huxley's word, changes in the physical world.

The efficacy of prayer tells us something so important about who we are and how the universe works that the rational mind can only gape. When a person *gets* this, *really gets it,* he or she might reasonably expect that massive studies of this phenomenon will be launched at any moment. Yet, along with other well-known but mysterious phenomena of human consciousness—intuition, say, or telepathy, or clairvoyance—prayer and its effects have long been considered to lie somewhere beyond the descriptions of science. And so prayer is not usually a feature of scientific conversations, even—or especially—in the realm of the healing professions.

Recently I attended a psychiatric grand-rounds presentation at our local hospital that makes the point. The subject of
the well-attended noontime talk was the treatment of post-
traumatic stress disorder. PTSD is a relatively new diagnostic
label first coined to describe long-lasting thought and mood
disturbances reported by veterans of the Vietnam War. The
diagnosis has since been expanded to describe persistent states
of distress reported by adults or children who have been
confronted by violence, serious injury, or death.

The presenting psychiatrist was an earnest person, con-
versational in his tone. He showed several slides of numbers
and graphs, all part of a research study funded by a drug company, that indicated the relative effectiveness or ineffectiveness
of several psychotropic drugs.

In one slide, the curve that represented improvement in a
group of patients who had been given one of the psychotropic
drugs looked about the same as the curve representing the
improvement in a group who had been given placebos. I wondered if he would say something about the effectiveness of placebos and the questions they raise about the relationship of the
mind and physiological change. But he didn't. Another slide
seemed to confirm the merits of "exposure therapy," a new
piece of nomenclature I hadn't heard before, which turned out
to mean when a client tells the story of the traumatizing event
to a therapist.

There was no mention of prayer. This omission, though
not surprising, is all the more telling as Vietnam vets suffering from PTSD are forming support groups of their own to
share their stories with each other. They are speaking publicly

about the politics of recovery—about the healing effects of prayer, the helpfulness of the recovery movement, and the life-changing effects of revisiting Vietnam in a devout spirit of reconciliation.

But changes are coming.

Prayer studies are difficult to design and easy to criticize, but more and more they are seeing the light of day. In his best-selling book *Healing Words: The Power of Prayer and the Practice of Medicine,* physician and author Larry Dossey writes stirringly about silent prayer, unconscious prayer, prayers that are answered before they are made. He tells about experimental trials of what is being called "distant intentionality" on just about every living thing you can think of, including germinating seeds and modest creatures like bacteria and yeast. From a number of well-respected research centers, a growing body of documentation suggests that prayerful intention can promote growth and healing in coronary patients, AIDS patients, premature infants, and surgical cases—and it can do it in the absence of direct sensory contact.

In a celebrated experiment at San Francisco General Hospital, described for lay readers in a *Saturday Evening Post* article by Dossey, cardiologist Randolph Byrd recruited people from around the country to pray for roughly half of his 393 patients. These were people who had been admitted to the coronary care unit with frank heart attacks or severe chest pain. Neither the patients nor their physicians and nurses knew who was being prayed for and who wasn't. In the group of people who were prayed for, there were fewer deaths, a significant reduction in the need for potent medication, and no one required mechanical breathing support.

In addition to studies on the effects of prayerful *intention*, adventurous studies have been designed to measure the effects of more passive human *attention*. In one such study, an audience watching a stage performance was monitored by nearby random-number generators. These are little gadgets that tick off random sequences of numbers and register any deviations in these random patterns that may result from changes in energy or "resonance" in the room. In this study and others like it, deviations in these patterns increased during periods of high emotional content in the stage performance, suggesting a recordable change in the ambient resonance when the audience participants—unaware of the experiment—were in a state of rapt attention.

Recently I attended a more complex event hosted by San Francisco's Grace Cathedral that was to be a children's choral recital, a healing ceremony, and a scientific experiment looking for evidence of "collective resonance," all in one.

The event unfolded on the cathedral's softly lit indoor labyrinth, where a small chorus of children performed sacred chants and canons for a boy of fourteen who had suffered a cerebral hemorrhagic stroke. He was sitting in the middle of the labyrinth with his mother—she with her hand on his knee, he with his hand on her hand—while the researcher sat off to the side with a little black random-number generator.

The children's voices were pure, angel-pure, and when the event was over, tears were streaming down the teenager's cheeks, and his mother's too. Tears were streaming down all our cheeks. As it happened, the little black gadget failed that day, so we don't know what it would have said. But we know what the boy said. "I've never had such an experience of something resonating through me like that," he told us, "sitting there under that *light.*"

In Grace Cathedral we find ourselves in a farther realm. Out past the edges of conventional research, we are in the netherworld of the miraculous. After all, we have been taught to ask, where is the scientific proof? Where is the repeatability? Back on Earth, where the more common therapeutic event involves the prescribing of pills, this past-the-edges world is still a terrifically controversial place.

Larry Dossey makes the controversy vivid with a story from the early days of his own medical career, a story that speaks of the still-repressive backdrop of classical science in the treatment world and the way it becomes internalized in the practitioner.

As a young doctor, Dossey had a hospital patient who was dying of metastatic lung cancer and had chosen to forgo all further medical and surgical care. And so he was sent home to die, where his only treatment was around-the-clock prayer by members of his church. A year later, Dossey learned his patient was back in the hospital, very much alive but suffering from a routine case of the flu. Dossey rushed to the radiology department to view the latest chest X ray and read the radiologist's report. The note on the film, referring to the patient's history of lung cancer, read, "In the intervening twelve months, there has been a dramatic response to therapy."

"I knew what the radiologist did not know," Dossey tells us. "The only therapy was prayer."

Unnerved, he sought out two medical school professors to ask them what they thought had happened. When their responses amounted to something like, "This happens sometimes," Dossey confesses, "I did what most doctors do when confronted with these inexplicable phenomena: I ignored it. It took me many years to gather enough courage to confront these events without cringing."

Maybe we are a little like the Patagonians, Dossey suggests—those folks on the beach who were able to see the rowboats of Darwin's landing party but were blind to the inconceivably large brigantine, *Beagle,* anchored just offshore. Here on our own beach, the healing effects of prayer are too hard to reconcile with what we have been taught is ascertainable, "scientific," and therefore true. Rowboats we get; brigantines we don't.

great metaphors & analogies

Creation is ever appearing, and must continue to appear from the nature of its inexhaustible source.
> Mary Baker Eddy,
> *Science and Health*

DICK OLNEY WOULD SOMETIMES recite this lovely prayer:
I give thanks for help unknown, already on the way.

The words just came to him one day, he said, and I saw him use them to wonderful effect with people in his workshops. There is something about this *already.* Everything just stops, and the breath becomes expectant, even—or especially—in moments of great need. Dick's prayer concedes the mysteries of space and time; it "fractalizes" a person. And it accomplishes all of this in ten words.

A client of mine devised a prayer that accomplished it in two. Her story invites questions about what a prayer is and isn't, and it also raises a dilemma.

ONE MORNING, she clumped in on her crutches, her left foot in a graying knee-high cast. She parked her crutches against a chair, eased herself down onto the sofa, and carefully lifted her casted leg into a nest of piled-up pillows. A small battery-driven myostimulator was strapped to her cast, blinking green as it sent periodic electrical impulses into her leg. Ruefully, she surveyed the scene.

Then she surprised me.

"You're not going to believe it. After all of this," she said, indicating her paraphernalia with a sweep of her hand, "the idea of getting my cast off is really scaring me."

She had broken a bone in her foot a few weeks earlier—a Jones fracture, tricky to heal short of surgery—and she had been grounded indefinitely from the world of equestrian competition, where she makes her living, and from serious volleyball. She missed her activities terribly. Without them, she'd been saying in her sessions, "I'm not even sure who I am." Impatient for the day the cast would come off, she had been working hard with sports medicine consultants on a several-times daily regimen of strengthening exercises and healing visualizations.

She had originally come into therapy with a clear goal in mind. She had broken up with a person she had been with for quite a while. "I want to clean up the part of me that keeps being attracted to people who are wounded," she had said then. "It took me way too long to figure out this guy didn't bring as much to the table as I did. Finally, I got tired of it, and I'm doing better with the breakup than I thought I would. But my confidence in choosing people is pretty shaky."

Then, shortly after she broke her foot, something happened that she hadn't expected. She met someone she liked very much, and he liked her. It had been a peculiar courtship, though, if it could be called a courtship at all, and maddening. Her injury slowed her down to the point that her life was almost unrecognizable to her, and she had to ask the people around her, including this new person, for help in doing the most trivial things. Asking for help was new for her, and she made no bones about not liking it. Her mother has struggled with Hodgkin's disease, thankfully in remission now, and my client considers herself more practiced in caring for people than in being cared for.

"This is not fun," she'd been saying. "I am damn well going to get better."

On this particular morning, though, she was not fitful or impatient or anything like it.

"Something has been happening this week," she said, looking out the window at something farther away than the curbside trees. "Maybe I've finally accepted the slowdown. There's been a new softness to everything—an acceptance of myself and other people." It was as if she were seeing this through the window. "I think I've always been patient, probably more patient with other people than with myself, and I've always been strong. Maybe because my mom was so sick. But this is something deeper than patience . . . something more strong than strong."

Her words were slow and wondering, and I found myself slowing down too, replaying the way she'd cozied a place for her leg in the pillows when she came in. Something had changed from the week before.

She sat back in the deep of the sofa, still gazing out. After a while she came back into the room and looked down at her toes as they peeked out from the cast. She hitched herself up a little straighter.

"Okay, let's see if I can describe this," she said. Everything in the room sat up a little straighter. Her voice seemed to say, "This is incredibly meaningful to me, and I don't know what it means."

"Since I can't put any weight on this foot," she began, "I have had to slow way down and concentrate on everything I do. When I crutch along, or go down stairs, or step out of the car onto my good leg, I've been saying cue words out loud to help myself pay attention to my footing. I've been saying, 'Ground-down. Ground-down.' Like a mantra."

She hesitated, looking for the right words.

"And I've been noticing that the ground feels . . . *different*. The ground seems to *feel me*. It's like . . . I'm stepping with intention, and the ground . . . the ground *acknowledges* my intention. It acknowledges that I'm not skimming. Skimming, like skating over my life. I used to have all these dreams about skating in college. Not skating like ice skating, but skating, like cruising over the top of things and not paying attention."

She glanced up to see if I was following.

Nodding, I was thinking how different this mantra was from the hard-edged, "I'm damn well going to get better." How her self-instruction, "Ground-down," in the moment it was answered, had become a prayer.

"It seems like your impatience about being 'grounded' has taken a turn," I told her. I couldn't resist the pun.

She indulged me with a little smile, but I'd interrupted her. "Grounded," she said, finding her way back to her fledgling story. "Amazing. The ground . . . it's . . . benevolent. It's always there—it's *there already*. Supporting me. Supporting growth and grace and harmony."

She smiled again. This time it was a smile with a sense of finish. "Who would have predicted this from a broken foot?"

There was a fine feeling of celebration in the room.

But, after only a minute, a cloud came over the sun.

"It's starting to make sense to me now," she said, "why getting my cast off is so scary."

We both knew this was the dilemma. How can she hold onto her tender awareness of a ground *there already* as she comes back into what we sometimes call the real world? Or is this even the right question? Maybe we don't "hold on" to epiphanies. Maybe they change us more subtly than that. Still, we worry, faithless, not wanting to be as we were before.

She looked up and asked sharply, "Am I going to lose this?"

The universe begins to look more like a great thought. . . .

Sir James Jeans,
The Mysterious Universe

"BUT EPIPHANIES DON'T LAST!" a friend of mine complains. She and I are walking down at the bay, talking about these things. "There is more to life than epiphanies!"

Forever true to her Scots-Irish forebears, she fixes me with a look.

"How do we move from epiphany states to knowing that we don't know anything?" she challenges me. "How do we accept that both are happening all the time? That both are holy?"

Of course, she is right. On a lucky day, we have our epiphanies, but we wonder, *What does any of this have to do with how I live my life?* We warp in and out of our realizations, saying, "I can't walk around believing what I believe all the time."

My friend is a psychotherapist too, and she shares an interest in the work of the physicist David Bohm. One of the most fascinating figures of twentieth-century science, Bohm offered particularly compelling imagery of a universe in which consciousness and Consciousness are in constant play.

Early in his career, Bohm moved from twin-particle work to the study of subatomic particles in gas and metallic systems. Each particle in these complex systems was found to behave in concert with its trillions of neighbors in something like a great, self-knowing electronic sea. Another remarkable discovery that seemed to resonate with these findings was made by the chaos theorist Leon Glass, who discovered that extremely small pieces of chicken embryo hearts, when shaken together in some kind of gruesome cocktail mixer, spontaneously began to beat in unison. There was beginning to be talk of "laws of chaos" operating in both living and nonliving systems.

Laws of chaos? Along with Bohm, the Nobel Prize—winning Belgian chemist Ilya Prigogine was puzzling about what sort of chaos this might be. It had long been believed that something less ordered can't evolve toward something more ordered. A scattered deck of cards doesn't reorganize itself, sorted now into suits; a broken-down sandpile doesn't reconfigure itself into a castle. But Prigogine found some examples of chemicals in nature moving surprisingly from disordered to more-ordered configurations. He called these self-organizing systems "dissipative structures."

"Dissipative structures." Too bad. If he had called them "spontaneous new forms," they might be a little easier for some of us to imagine. Whatever their name, Prigogine wondered if these surprising, "irregular" events were arising from a previously unsuspected order in "chaos." At the same time, Bohm, who was struggling to reconcile the two great disparate themes of twentieth-century physics—Einstein's general theory of relativity, which still sees separateness in the universe, and quantum mechanics, which sees an underlying connectedness—proposed a cosmos that might accommodate both.

Suppose, Bohm said, that within the "explicate" world we know so well there exists an "implicate" source world that eludes our physical senses because it is *not material*. This implicate world would be much like Aristotle's and Newton's chaos, invisible and unmanifested, evolving in response to feedback from the explicate world. Out of this infinitely vast source world, which pervades all of space-time, seemingly differentiated features of our familiar, "explicate" manifestations would rise up and fall back again, like waves on water. And if these differentiated features of our daily lives seem to be separate, and *are* in some way separate—separate photons, separate blades of grass, separate thoughts—this separateness is ultimately an illusion that belies the ultimate wholeness of the implicate/explicate interplay.

Sometime later, Bohm seemed to invoke this interplay in a conversation about human consciousness with the spiritual teacher Krishnamurti. "The pure energy of mind is able to reach into the limited energy of man," he says, sounding as if he is speaking of an implicate sea and its waves.

"And change the limitation," Krishnamurti says.

"Yes, that's right," Bohm agrees.

. . .

"GROUND DOWN," my client says. She calls these "cue words," and at first she uses them to help herself pay attention to her footing as she crutches along. Suddenly something happens she had not thought to ask for—the ground answers before it is asked. "Always here," it says, in response to a prayer not quite made. "Here *already.*"

This news exceeds our wildest hopes.

Then, crazily, we are back in the world again, asking, "Am I going to lose this?"

But surely this place where the two realms meet for a moment—this disorienting, beguiling, "Am-I-going-to-lose-this?"

place—this is the most interesting place of all. Standing here at the point where they touch, one can see into both realms and see oneself seeing. Later—even in forgetfulness, even when there is only the remnant of puzzlement—nothing will be quite the same.

Sometime later my client would write about her experience. "My realization," she writes, "was that the things I had been trying to 'skate over,' or ignore, or minimize in my life were not lying in wait for me, not in some sinister way. Quite the opposite. When I actually slowed down, and sat, and stared at the wall, my resources to deal with the challenges in my life were even bigger and more bountiful than I had ever dared to imagine. They were just waiting for me to be still and recognize them. The fear of getting my cast off had to do with worrying that I would lose sight of my resources/strength/power/okayness as the swirl and rip of my life took over again."

But nothing is quite the same again. With prayer we take ourselves to the edges of the mind—we do it on purpose—and there we are met. "It's benevolent," my client says of the ground under her step. In the gigantic landscape of the universe, this meeting is personal, memorable, inviting future prayers.

"Couldn't epiphanies be prayers from the implicate offered up into the explicate order?" my Scots-Irish friend asks as we walk along the water. "Maybe the 'implicate' is as lonely for us as we are for it. Maybe all of life is prayer—attempts of the universe to know itself as one."

HOMECOMING

If that happened to me, it has happened to others,
and I take it as a fact of human experience.

FLORIDA SCOTT-MAXWELL,
THE MEASURE OF MY DAYS

ONE NEW YEAR'S DAY, at the home of some friends at
Point Reyes, I pulled a chair over to a floor-to-ceiling
window to read and look out. A magnificent winter storm,
carrying along heavy winds and rain, had barreled in from
Hawaii like a 1,500-mile-long freight train and slammed into
the Northern California coast. They were calling it the Pine-
apple Express. It had been raining heavily and blowing hard,
on and off, for several days. Oddly, the temperature was
Hawaii mild and would have been inviting, soft, but this afternoon's gale winds were keeping me inside.

From my window, I could look down on Tomales Bay and
the concentric horizons of green mountains beyond, but as I
settled in, the long view was becoming obscured by heavy

clouds churning below me. A cozy fire was snapping in the stone fireplace, and I was seized with a strong physical memory of being in the red cabin at Silver Bay while a summer storm crashed outside the French doors that looked down on the bay. I closed my book.

The trees here on the Inverness ridge were bending over double in the blast, and small branches and pieces of lichen flew through the thick air, sometimes cracking sharply against the house. Ravens lifted up out of the tallest trees and tested the wind patterns. They flew hard into the strong currents and then fell back, like kayackers playing in white water.

Abruptly, the wind fell off. Clouds continued to boil in the exotic, tropical air, but slowly now, and more clouds rose up from the saturated slope in front of me—weather forming as I watched.

I thought about my wonderings at Silver Bay, about the metaphysics of a sun that is always there and clouds that only seem to hide it. How I had struggled to understand those metaphysical clouds!

Suddenly, in the eerie stillness here on the ridge, I imagined a cloud emanating from myself. It was as if I could see a small figure of myself with weather rising up out of me and forming above my head. I could see others too. I could see how their weather rises up, affecting mine and mine affecting theirs. I watched our systems of weather bumping into each other, running together.

Wow, I thought. All of us making our own weather.

I tried playing around. I looked for particular people in my life—family members, friends, clients. From here, I could see them living their lives in relation to the weather they were making. I could see the compelling details—doing things, deciding things, joy, and sorrow. But I saw that they were not their weather and I was not mine, although it usually seems so.

Then I imagined what it would be like if we could be together out here, free from the clouds we generate. So different! There were no judgments in this place, no stories. Only a certain texture, an exquisite love. Under the influence of our weather, even as we try to investigate our weather—in therapy, say—so much is unseen.

My God, I thought. We know so little!

It seemed to me the tragedy of this should break my heart. The absurdity of it, the suffering.

But strangely, my heart was not breaking. Instead, I found myself marveling at the courage it takes to live in weather, engrossed in the details and dramas of everyday life. And marveling at the relief so close at hand.

"It is not that we are material beings trying to be spiritual," the Dalai Lama has said, "but that we are spiritual beings trying to be material."

The winter afternoon was dusky purple now. The storm outside was gathering force again, and pieces from the battered trees were flying against the house. The sound of things crashing brought me back, and the awe I had been experiencing gave way to some apprehension as the howling wind swirled all around me in the fading light.

Years have passed, but this experience has stayed with me strongly. In my practice, I have sometimes suggested to clients that they think of the circumstances of their lives—the good news and bad news—as weather passing over. Who would they be, separate from their weather? But it was not until that stormy afternoon on the ridge that I saw how we, like the earth itself, make our own weather—it seems to be in the nature of things—and how easy it is to confuse it with something more permanent about ourselves.

· · ·

ONE MORNING, a client I spoke of early in this book arrived for her session, talking fast as she came through the door. She backed into the chair and kept on talking, hardly taking time to breathe. It had been two weeks since I had seen her, and all the hard things that had been happening—daunting things— were spilling out in a rush. There was a brother in jail, a father drunk on Easter morning, a mother fallen ill.

"And my sister," she said. "Usually I can count on her, but she's been acting seriously out to lunch."

So much. So much trouble.

Her report went on, rapid-fire, for maybe half an hour. She looked thin to me, and her face was pinched. Her eyes scrubbed the carpet near her feet, back and forth.

Finally she seemed to come to the end of it. She looked up.

"I've written a letter to my sister in my mind," she said, her words a little slower now.

Maybe she would like to "read" it to me, I thought. Maybe there is something in it that we would find helpful. Then, before I could ask her to read her letter, something changed. She stopped talking, stopped short, and settled back into her chair.

I was not so settled in my own chair. For the first time in the session, there was room for me to say something, but nothing came. She sat with her eyes half closed, while I, with my own eyes half closed, tried to imagine how I could possibly be of any help to her this morning. What did I really know about any of this?

Silence.

Then the air in the room seemed to freshen, as if a weather front had passed through. I sensed that her breathing had changed, and when I looked up, I was amazed to find that her face had taken on an inquiring look and, as I watched, was breaking into a wide, pink-cheeked grin. It was a grin I had not seen before.

"I feel something," she said, in a wondering sort of way. She reached around with her hand to see if she could locate it. "It's an opening back here above my buttocks. You know where Dennis the Menace's pajama flap is unbuttoned? Light is streaming into me!"

As brilliant as her face had become, I might have missed it. Intent on helping her, I had been holding out for the letter to her sister.

The room was completely different now, awash in a clear light that seemed to bleach out her anxious story, along with my own tired impulse to help her, like a couple of overexposed photographs.

She looked at me with steady eyes. "It's a miracle," she said in a new voice. "I'm perfectly all right."

I drew my hand through the fine texture of light in the room. It felt slightly viscous.

It was a long time before either of us spoke.

"Perfectly all right," she said again.

They are phenomena, nothing more.
Miracles are just part of the whole truth.

Spyros Sathi,
twentieth-century Christian mystic

A MIRACLE! As fierce as a hurricane, as delicate as a dande-
lion gone to silver seed!

The world's mystics have always exclaimed there is nothing miraculous about miracles. They happen, St. Augustine
said, "not in opposition to Nature, but in opposition to what
we know of Nature."

Other times, other cultures have taken more kindly to
miracles than our own. When I asked a colleague, trained in
the venerable Japanese art of Jin Shin Jyutso, about the place
where my client experienced the light streaming into her, she
was unfazed. "Oh yes," she said. "In the Eastern system, that's
where the cosmic light steps down and enters the cellular
body. The nonmanifested or premanifested order of creation,
when it manifests, steps down into each realm—the physical,
mental, and emotional."

Our own North American neighbors are unfazed too. For
the Inuit people, the Arctic winter—which I used to think
must be a long, cold wait in the dark—is the time for sacred
feasts and dances. Wearing costumes and masks that look as
they did in prehistoric times, the people sing, "Could it not be
that the world we see around us is the reflection of another,
hidden universe?"

In Mexico during the holiest Festival of the Virgin, She,
the olive-skinned One, joins people of all skins, light and dark,
to each other and to God. It is said that as the old people leave

the church on this night of the Virgin, they cannot take their eyes off the church doors. And so they walk backwards.

They walk backwards.

Oh, I envy our neighbors, dancing in winter's darkness, walking backwards in the night, while we in the world of psychotherapy still struggle with our secular tradition.

Freud, who called himself "godless," mulled questions about metaphysics and religion throughout his life. In his office he kept a collection of idols and animal gods from a variety of indigenous cultures. But he steadfastly wrote that religious ideas arise from an infantile impulse to defend against the whimsies of an indifferent universe. Ongoing reliance on religion amounts to magical or dependent thinking, he said, and indicates a person's developmental arrest.

And so psychotherapy, laboring under weather of its own, went down a certain road, depriving itself of a much wider sacred tradition. And when my client has an intimation of something coming from outside her familiar world, her experience— which is about to change everything—is at risk. This is obviously not because she and I are not interested in healing, but we might worry about how valid or "rational" her experience is or whether it belongs more properly in a place of worship than in the therapy room. We might miss it completely.

Yet—seemingly against all odds—these grace-filled moments keep coming, pushing through our orthodoxies and reminding us of their transformative power. "Light is streaming into me!" she exclaims, surprising us both, and we are transported out to the place beyond personal weather, where the universe makes itself known to us.

The happy word "serendipity" captures this moment of recognition. Though it is sometimes used to mean a lucky accident or the coming together of seemingly unrelated events, Horace Walpole, the eighteenth-century English novelist, actually coined the word to mean the human attribute or faculty for apprehending the surprising and marvelous.

In his telling of the ancient tale "The Three Princes of Serendip," Walpole tells us, "As their highnesses traveled, they were always making discoveries of things they were not in quest of." Traveling with these young princes, we encounter a purposeful and benevolent universe, and they, in turn, are endowed with serendipity, which will sustain and guide them in all their journeys.

The English biologist Rupert Sheldrake captures this exchange, too, in his conjectures about the extraordinary powers of ordinary animals and other mysteries close at hand. Sheldrake is fascinated by such seemingly homely questions as, "How do dogs know when their owners are returning home?" and "How do pigeons home?"

One time I heard him tell an anecdotal story about some little birds called blue tits, who learned a new behavior—and that's not all. The story goes that in 1921, in Southhampton, England, a woman was startled one morning to see a blue tit light down on a bottle of milk that had been delivered to her front porch, pull off the cap with its beak, and drink some of the cream. Other villagers were soon remarking that they were seeing this curious behavior too. There were even reports of parties of tits following the milkman down the street and mobbing the milk bottles on his truck. It seemed the blue tits were teaching each other a new trick.

An analysis of records kept in England from 1930 to 1947 shows that the spread of this habit accelerated as time went on. But it also suggests, because blue tits are known to venture only a few miles from their nesting place, that it was independently discovered by individual blue tits at least eighty-nine times in the British Isles. It also appeared among tits in Sweden, Denmark, and Holland.

The Dutch records are of particular interest to Sheldrake. With the coming of World War II, milk delivery was discontinued. Then, the moment delivery resumed, blue tits all over the countryside were observed pulling off bottle caps and drinking the cream. But here's the catch: The generation of blue tits who invented the trick had long since died off. How did the postwar birds in Holland know?

Sheldrake uses this story and others to suggest that nature has a memory. This memory is conveyed nonlocally through time and space by what he calls "morphic fields" that shape everything in our living universe—an atom's atomness, a jaguar's jaguarness, a blue tit's blue-titness. Suppose a jaguar's jaguarness is not contained locally in its genes but nonlocally in its morphic field, which is then downloaded by its genes. Suppose this is a two-way flow of information. Suppose the local knowledge of a few English blue tits can make its way back to nonlocal blue-titness—that blue-titness can learn and evolve, download these learnings to other blue tits, and so on.

A FEW EXCEPTIONAL EXAMPLES
ARE EVIDENCE FOR A
UNIVERSAL PHENOM?

Sheldrake also tells a story about a simple human experiment devised by an undergraduate student in the department of psychology at the University of Nottingham. The student asked two groups of participants to work a crossword puzzle, one before and one after it was published in the daily Nottingham newspaper. She reasoned that if memory is nonlocal and can learn, the more people who learn a task, the easier it should be for others to do. The hypothesis predicts that the second group will have an easier time with the puzzle after it's been published, and that's what she found to be true.

. . .

WE ARE ALL LOOKING for something. We are looking with everything we've got. And we've been looking since the beginning of time. Before that.

Sometimes, probably most of the time, we don't quite know we're looking—we're just doing what we're doing, or waking up tired. Sometimes we know beyond the shadow of a doubt.

Then there comes a moment when our looking for something just stops, when the looked-for something appears or reveals that it has been there all along. There is a softening to it, a flush of recognition. Knowing again.

Knowing what again? There is not much discussion in therapeutic circles about this moment, not much written. If it comes into the room as a surprise, incongruent with a person's usual experience, what is it congruent with? What does it tell us about who we really are and where we live? And why are we not gathering in the center of town to talk about it?

As a young girl, I felt the longing piercingly. Up on my elbows in the loft window on Silver Bay, I would stare out into the terrifying beauty of the night sky, looking for some reason for myself, fighting like bloody hell the long fall into no reason.

Then, out on the raft, I would have that seemingly accidental and utterly convincing experience of slipping out past my thoughts, past my awful nighttime wonderings, into the arms of a living universe. This was more than a momentary fulfillment of longing; it was a homecoming.

"Show me everything!" was my exuberant thought. "I want to know." And it came to me then that wanting to know *was* the reason for me—that the universe is in lively contemplation of itself. I and what I am looking at are the same; I and what I am looking for are the same.

I never doubted the truth of these homecomings out on the raft. But—as I rowed the boat back, tied up to the pier, and climbed the hill to the cabin—they thinned out. The so-called real world of family and mosquitoes and what's for dinner reasserted itself and persuaded me that's where I needed to be. My experiences never quite made it into stories that I told myself or anyone, and what I knew . . . I didn't know, not all the way.

Moving back and forth between longing and homecoming—taking one as an intimation of the other—is, it seems to me, what it is to be a person. Out in the open we see all the way to heaven. Then something closes in again, like weather.

Still, our longings whisper.

The other day I heard Edgar Mitchell, the Apollo XIV astronaut and founder of the Institute of Noetic Sciences, tell the story of the epiphany he experienced out beyond the weather. Returning home from the moon, Mitchell was gazing out of the window of *Apollo* at the jewel of Earth against the backdrop of a cosmos still spraying out into unimaginable depths of space. Awestruck, he saw that the seemingly separate elements of the universe are deeply and purposefully interconnected, and in the same moment he saw that this great paradox is comprehensible to human consciousness.

Of his revelation he has written, "My mind was flooded with an intuitive knowing that we humans, both as individuals and as a species, are an integral part of the ongoing process of creation." In that moment—looking out, looking in—he was changed.

People don't usually come to psychotherapy asking for a trip to the moon, not exactly. People come feeling there is something wrong with them or with the world. My morning client, besieged by so much trouble, is down to the letter she has written to her sister in her mind. But still she comes, expectant somehow, and, as we sit together, something happens that takes us both by surprise. "It's a miracle," she says, as we sit in a light like the light that follows a storm. "I'm perfectly all right."

Moments of surprise come, compelling us with their grace, even when the problems of life seem too daunting to bear. Making room for our stories of epiphany—agreeing to tell them—we rivet our attention onto these moments, watch for the objections that conspire against them, and explore their power for healing.

"Look at this!" we say. "Look with me." And in the saying, we are changed, and so is the world.

NOTES AND

SUGGESTED READINGS

INTRODUCTION

p. 8. Reynolds Price, "A Single Meaning: Notes on the Origins and Life of Narrative," an introductory essay to be found in Price's book, *A Palpable God: Thirty Stories Translated from the Bible* (San Francisco: North Point Press, 1985) p. 18.

CHAPTER 1

p. 19. Mary Baker Eddy, *Science and Health with Key to the Scriptures* (Boston: The Christian Science Publishing Society, 1971) p. 392. *Science and Health* and the *Bible* are the textbooks of practicing Christian Scientists.

CHAPTER 2

p. 26. "Talk of the Nation: Science Friday," hosted by Ira Flatow, National Public Radio, June 26, 1992. Tapes and transcripts of "Science Friday" programs can be ordered by calling (877) NPR-TEXT.

p. 27. Bell's Theorem has been called "*the* most profound discovery of science" by the respected physicist Henry Stapp, University of California, Berkeley, in a paper entitled "Bell's Theorem and World

Process," *Il Nuovo Cimento,* 29B, 1975. For a discussion of the significance of this assertion, accessible to science majors and non-science majors alike, see Huston Smith's book *Beyond the Post-Modern Mind* (Wheaton, IL: Quest Books, 1989) p. 241.

p. 34. Larry Dossey, *Healing Words: The Power of Prayer and the Practice of Medicine* (San Francisco: HarperSanFrancisco, 1993). Dossey is the author of a number of thoughtful and inspirational books. He is currently the executive editor of the journal *Alternative Therapies in Health and Medicine.*

p. 36. Ralph Waldo Emerson, *Essays: First Series,* "Compensation," 1841.

p. 36. D. S. Kothari, "Atom and Self," *Proceedings of the Indian National Science Academy,* Part A, Physical Science, 46:1, 1980, p. 13. Larry Dossey dedicates his book, *Meaning and Medicine: Lessons from a Doctor's Tales of Breakthrough and Healing* (New York: Bantam Books, 1991) to Professor Kothari. In his acknowledgments Dossey writes, "'Atom and Self'. . . is one of the most profound discussions of the mind-body problem I have ever discovered."

CHAPTER 3

p. 41. "A temporary expedient." It *was* Bell. See Paul Davies and J. R. Brown (eds), *The Ghost in the Atom* (Cambridge: Cambridge University Press, 1986). Bell and other physicists interviewed for a BBC Radio series are struggling to make sense of their findings.

p. 41. Ken Wilber, ed., *Quantum Questions: Mystical Writings of the World's Great Physicists* (Boston: Shambala, 1985).

p. 42. For more discussion of human consciousness by Roger Penrose, including more on microtubules for those inclined, see Roger Penrose, *Shadows of the Mind: A Search for the Missing Science of Consciousness* (New York: Oxford University Press, 1994). See also John Horgan, *The Undiscovered Mind: How the Human Brain Defies Replication, Medication and Explanation* (New York: Touchstone, 1999), an irreverent and helpful tour of the realm of mind science that concludes with an enigmatic and provocative personal story.

p. 44. "Premodern, modern, postmodern." For a majestic intellectual history of the Western world, treat yourself to Richard Tarnas, *The Passion of the Western Mind: Understanding the Ideas That Have Shaped Our WorldView* (New York: Ballantine Books, 1991). In his epilogue, Tarnas makes a case for the evolution through time of human consciousness.

p. 45. For biographies of these theory builders of the Scientific Revolution, I am indebted to *Encyclopedia Britannica,* Fifteenth Edition, 1977, and to my children who, over the years, lost only one volume of it.

p. 52. Neil Levy is a friend and neighbor. Sometimes an analysis like this comes out of his mouth, leaving him looking quite surprised. For original tales that illuminate portions of the *Torah,* watch for his new book, *The Last Rebbe of Bialystok* (Berkeley, CA: Creative Arts Book Co., in publication).

p. 52. The colleague who worked with this sister and brother, and who contributes the Picasso story, is my own brother, Richard Trumbull—the same brother who hunted frogs with Freddie Hutchinson. For references to his work, see bibliography.

p. 53. Sir James Jeans, *The Mysterious Universe* (Cambridge, England: Cambridge University Press, 1931) p. 111.

CHAPTER 4

p. 59. Herbert Benson, *Timeless Healer: The Power and Biology of Belief* (New York: Scribner, 1997).

p. 64. "Experimental control." See, Neil S. Jacobson, "Contextualism Is Dead: Long Live Contextualism," *Family Process,* Vol. 33, No. 1, March 1994.

p. 64. Michael White and David Epston, *Narrative Means to Therapeutic Ends* (New York: W. W. Norton, 1990). This trailblazing book from Down Under amounts to a wholly new look at problems, therapy, power, meaning, and the re-authoring of person's life.

p. 65. For an intriguing essay about an enigmatic Isaac Newton, read David Kubrin, "Newton's Inside Out!" in Henry Woolf, ed., *The Analytic Spirit: Essays in the History of Science* (Ithaca, NY: Cornell University Press, 1990).

p. 69. "The most brilliant mind since Aristotle," said Albert Einstein. "One of the last of the magi," said Lord Keynes. (See David Kubrin's essay, above.) One of the men who asserted the materialist program into existence, says Theodore Roszak. In his book *The Voice of the Earth* (New York: Simon and Schuster, 1992), Roszak offers an urgent and erudite analysis of modern psychology "in search of its soul" and his proposal for a more holistic "ecopsychology." Roszak includes a rich annotated bibliographic appendix, "God and Modern Cosmology."

p. 72. Jon Kabat-Zinn, *Full Catastrophe Living: Using the Wisdom of Your Body and Mind to Face Stress, Pain, and Illness* (New York: Delta Books, 1990). This compassionate book is more often on loan than on my shelf.

CHAPTER 5

p. 83. Bruno Bettelheim, *Freud and Man's Soul* (New York: Alfred A. Knopf, 1983).

p. 96. Mary S. Wylie, "Diagnosing for Dollars?" *Networker,* May / June 1995.

CHAPTER 6

p. 99. Kiwi Tamasese is a member of the therapy team of the Family Center, Lower Hutt, New Zealand. This quote comes from a story she tells from her Pacific Island tradition.

p. 99. As quoted in Lawrence Weschler's essay, "True to Life," an introduction to David Hockney, *Cameraworks* (New York: Alfred A. Knopf, 1984) p. 23.

pp. 101–102. Vaclav Havel, "Address at Independence Hall," July 4, 1994. Full text available on Op Ed page, *New York Times,* July 8, 1994, and in *Utne Reader,* Jan-Feb 1995.

p. 105. See Lynn Hoffman, *Foundations of Family Therapy: A Conceptual Framework for Systems Change* (New York: Basic Books, 1981). Hoffman's elegant text is mandatory reading for an understanding of the history and significance of family therapy and for the importance of the contributions of Gregory Bateson, Virginia Satir and others at the Mental Research Institute of Palo Alto. See also her essay, "Constructing Realities," *Family Process*, 29, 1, March 1990, pp. 1-12.

pp. 106–107. For an excellent introduction to theory and practice in the psychoanalytic tradition, see Harry Guntrip, *Psychoanalytic Theory, Therapy, and the Self: A Basic Guide to the Human Personality in Freud, Erikson, Klein, Sullivan, Fairbairn, Hartmann, Jacobson, and Winnicott* (New York: Basic Books, 1973).

To read contributors to these traditions in their own voices, see:

Jordan, Judith V., Alexandra G. Kaplan, Jean Baker Miller, Irene P. Stiver, Janet L. Surrey, *Women's Growth in Connection* (New York: Guilford Press, 1991).

Kernberg, Otto, *Borderline Conditions and Pathological Narcissism* (New York: Jason Aronson, Inc., 1975).

Kohut, Heinz, *The Restoration of the Self* (New York: International Universities Press, 1977).

Napier, Augustus and Carl Whitaker, *The Family Crucible: The Intense Experience of Family Therapy* (New York: HarperCollins, 1988). This narrative of a family in therapy reads like a warm-hearted novel, hard to put down.

Weiss, Joseph and Harold Sampson, *How Psychotherapy Works: Process and Technique* (New York: Guilford Press, 1993).

Winnicott, D. W., *The Maturational Processes and the Facilitating Environment: Studies in the Theory of Emotional Development* (New York: International Universities Press, 1965). And *Through Pediatrics to Psychoanalysis* (New York: Basic Books, 1975). Read Adam Phillips' essays (reference below) for fond discussions of Winnicott's work.

p. 108. Elizabeth Lloyd Mayer, "The Essential Subjectivity and Intersubjectivity of Clinical Facts," *International Journal of Psychoanalysis,* 77:4, 1996, p. 718. See also Mayer, *Extraordinary Knowing: Making Sense of the Inexplicable in Everyday Life* (New York: Bantam Dell, in publication).

p. 108. White and Epston, 1990.

p. 115. Huston Smith, *Beyond the Post-Modern Mind,* (Wheaton, IL: Quest Books, 1989) p. 3.

p. 115. For more delights and surprises from Adam Phillips, see *On Kissing, Tickling and Being Bored: Psychoanalytic Essays on the Unexamined Life* (Cambridge, MA: Harvard University Press, 1994). The paper entitled "Psychoanalysis and the Future of Fear" appears as "Fear" in Phillips' *Terrors and Experts* (Cambridge, MA: Harvard University Press, 1996).

CHAPTER 7

p. 123. *Magic Eye: A New Way of Looking at the World,* 3D Illusions by N. E. Thing Enterprises (Kansas City: Andrews & McNeel, 1994).

p. 125. There are many books to be read about Albert Einstein. To hear him in his own voice, try two essays entitled "Cosmic Religious Feeling" and "Science and Religion," to be found in Ken Wilber's anthology, *Quantum Questions* (see above).

p. 126. See Werner Heisenberg, *Physics and Philosophy* (New York: Harper Torchbooks, 1958).

p. 131. If you have time to read only one book about the latest frontiers of physics, the paranormal abilities of the mind, and the human soul, it might be Michael Talbot's *The Holographic Universe* (New York: HarperCollins, 1991).

p. 132. For more of Davies, see *God and the New Physics* (New York: Simon & Schuster, 1984), and *The Mind of God: The Scientific Basis for a Rational World* (New York, Touchstone Books, 1993).

p. 132. See Penrose, 1994.

p. 133. Stephen Hawking, *A Brief History of Time* (New York: Basic Books, 1988). Hawking tried valiantly to make his book easy to read. It isn't.

CHAPTER 8

p. 141. Werner Heisenberg, 1958.

p. 141. Rupert Sheldrake, Terence McKenna, and Ralph Abraham, *The Evolutionary Mind: Trialogues at the Edge of the Unthinkable* (Santa Cruz, CA: Trialogue Press). This terrific book and an earlier one, *Trialogues at the Edge of the West: Chaos, Creativity and the Resacralization of the World,* 1992, can be hard to find. Try faxing (408) 425-7436. See also the newest in this trialogue series, *Chaos, Creativity, and Cosmic Consciousness,* with a foreword by Jean Houston (New York: Park Street Press, 2001).

p. 148. Dick Olney, *Walking in Beauty* (Mendocino, CA: DO Publishing, 1996). Dick never wrote a book, but transcripts of his work, together with some of his best one-liners, poems, and ways of thinking about a person, have been collected by his students and are available here.

p. 151. Aldous Huxley, *The Perennial Philosophy* (New York: Harper-Collins, 1990).

p. 156. Huston Smith's many books are a light unto the world. One can't do without these two: *The World's Religions* (San Francisco: HarperSanFrancisco, 1991). And *Why Religion Matters: The Fate of the Human Spirit in an Age of Disbelief* (San Francisco: HarperSanFrancisco, 2001).

CHAPTER 9

p. 159. "God Speaks to the Soul," Mechthilde of Magdeburg, as found in Andrew Harvey, ed., *Teachings of the Christian Mystics* (Boston: Shambala, 1998).

p. 159. Aldous Huxley, *Doors of Perception* (New York: HarperCollins, 1990). And see Huston Smith, *Cleansing the Doors of Perception: The Religious Significance of Entheogenic Plants and Chemicals* (New York: Jeremy P. Tarcher/Putnam, 2000).

p. 162. Dossey, 1993.

p. 162. For the study mentioned, see: Larry Dossey, "Prayer is Good Medicine," *The Saturday Evening Post,* Nov/Dec, 1997, p. 52.

p. 163. For an inquiry into the effects of human attention and intention, see Dean Radin, *The Conscious Universe* (San Francisco: HarperSanFrancisco, 1997).

p. 164. The random number generator failed because the battery was dead. Surely the contrast of a scientific experiment at the far edge of the knowable and a dead battery is a wonder of its own.

p. 165. "Without cringing," Dossey, 1997, p. 52.

P. 165. Reference to the Patagonians, Larry Dossey, *Space, Time and Medicine* (Boston: Shambala, 1985) p. 10.

p. 170. For a reference to this work of Leon Glass in a dramatic exposition of a brand-new science, see James Gleick, *Chaos: Making a New Science* (New York: Viking, 1987) p. 305. See also Theodor Schwenk, *Sensitive Chaos: The Creation of Flowing Forms in Water and Air* (London: Rudolf Steiner Press, 1999). This beautiful book, wonderfully illustrated, is unfortunately out of print. Try the library.

p. 171. Ilya Prigogine and Isabelle Stengers, *Order Out of Chaos: Man's New Dialogue with Nature* (New York: Bantam Books, 1984). Prigogine puts the pieces that were left to us by the Scientific Age back together. See also M. Lukas, "The World According to Ilya Prigogine," *Quest/80,* December 1980, p. 88.

p. 171. David Bohm, *Wholeness and the Implicate Order* (London: Routledge & Kegan Paul, 1980).

p. 172. David Bohm and Krishnamurti, "The Future of Humanity," (New York: Mystic Fire Video, 1985). Call (800) 292-9001 for tape or catalog. A mind-bending conversation about suffering, insight, changes in brain cells, and the immateriality of matter, available on videotape.

CHAPTER 10

p. 180. The Greek mystic Spyros Sathi, known as Daskalos, was interviewed by Mark Matousek. See "The Teaching," *Common Boundary*, July/Aug 1995, p. 42. For more of Daskalos, see Kyriacos C. Markides, *The Magus of Strovolos: The Extraordinary World of a Spiritual Healer* (New York: Penguin/Arkana, 1990).

p. 180. My colleague is Diana Kehlmann, a practitioner of Jin Shin Jyutsu, an ancient Japanese practice of hands-on healing, which was brought to the United States by Mary Burmeister, a Japanese-American practitioner, after World War II. For an introduction to this holistic approach, see *The Touch of Healing: Energizing Body, Mind and Spirit with the Art of Jin Shin Jyutsu*, Alice Burmeister, et al. (New York: Bantam Books, 1997).

p. 180. As you walk through the Cosmology Gallery of the Royal British Columbia Museum, in Victoria, British Columbia, you hear these words from an audio script celebrating the Inuit cosmology: "All people believe that there is more to the universe than meets the eye. Modern wisdom makes certain distinctions; some things are considered imaginary, while others are thought to be real. Today we believe that the soul of man is far different than that of birds and animals. But, could it not be that the world we see around us is the reflection of another, hidden universe?"

p. 181. For a discussion of Freud's psychological-metaphysical impasse, read Adam Phillips' essay, "Psychoanalysis and Idolatry," in Phillips, 1994.

p. 182. This ancient tale, first told in English by Walpole in the eighteenth century, has been retold in a children's book with lovely drawings. See Elizabeth J. Hodges, *The Three Princes of Serendip* (New York: Atheneum, 1964).

p. 182. Ann Jauregui, "Three Tales from Serendip," *The Chrysalis Reader,* 2002, pp. 47–51.

pp. 182–183. For the blue tit story and an exposition of his radical theory of morphic resonance, see Rupert Sheldrake, *The Presence of the Past: Morphic Resonance and the Habits of Nature* (Rochester, VT: Park Street Press, 1995). See also Sheldrake, *Seven Experiments That Could Change the World: A Do-It-Yourself Guide to Revolutionary Science* (New York: Riverhead Books, 1995).

p. 184. Sheldrake reports the crossword puzzle experiment in the *Institute of Noetic Sciences Bulletin,* Autumn 1991, p. 1–3.

pp. 185–186. For the adventures of this Apollo astronaut, scientist, and mystic, see Edgar Mitchell, Dwight Williams (contributor), *The Way of the Explorer: An Apollo Astronaut's Journey Through the Material and Mystical Worlds* (New York: Putnam Publishing Group, 1996).

BIBLIOGRAPHY

Ammon, A. R. *Collected Poems, 1951–1971*. New York: Norton, 2001.

Bateson, Gregory. *Mind and Nature*. New York: Dutton, 1979.

———. *Steps to an Ecology of the Mind*. New York: Ballantine Books, 1972.

Bellah, Robert N., et al. *Habits of the Heart*. New York: HarperCollins, 1994.

Benson, Herbert. *Beyond the Relaxation Response*. New York: Times Books, 1984.

———. *Timeless Healer: The Power and Biology of Belief.* New York: Scribner, 1997.

Berry, Wendell. *What Are People For?* San Francisco: North Point Press, 1990.

———. *A World Lost*. Washington, D.C.: Counterpoint Press, 1996.

Bettelheim, Bruno. *Freud and Man's Soul*. New York: Alfred A. Knopf, 1983.

Blanck, Gertrude and Rubin Blanck. *Ego Psychology I: Psychoanalytic Developmental Psychology*. New York: Columbia University Press, 1974.

———. *Ego Psychology II: Psychoanalytic Developmental Psychology*. New York: Columbia University Press, 1994.

Bohm, David. *Unfolding Meaning.* New York: Arc Paperbacks, 1994.

―――. *Wholeness and the Implicate Order.* London: Routledge & Kegan Paul, 1980.

―――. *Causality and Chance in Modern Physics.* Philadelphia: University of Pennsylvania Press, 1971.

Bohm, David, and Krishnamurti. "The Future of Humanity." New York: Mystic Fire Video, 1985.

Burmeister, Alice, et al. *The Touch of Healing: Energizing Body, Mind and Spirit with the Art of Jin Shin Jyutsu.* New York: Bantam Books, 1997.

Capra, Fritjof. *The Turning Point.* New York: Bantam, 1982.

Chatwin, Bruce. *The Songlines.* London: Picador, 1988.

Chodron, Pema. *The Wisdom of No Escape.* Boston: Shambala, 1991.

Davies, Paul. *About Time.* New York: Simon & Schuster, 1995.

―――. *The Mind of God: The Scientific Basis for a Rational World.* New York: Touchstone Books, 1993.

―――. *God and the New Physics,* New York: Simon & Schuster, 1984.

Davies, Paul and J. R. Brown, eds. *The Ghost in the Atom.* Cambridge: Cambridge University Press, 1986.

Diagnostic and Statistical Manual of Mental Disorders, Fourth Edition, Washington, D.C.: American Psychiatric Association, 1995.

Dillard, Annie. *Pilgrim at Tinker Creek.* San Francisco: Perennial Library, 1985.

Dossey, Larry. *Healing Words: The Power of Prayer and the Practice of Medicine.* San Francisco: HarperSanFrancisco, 1993.

―――. *Meaning and Medicine: Lessons from a Doctor's Tales of Breakthrough and Healing.* New York: Bantam, 1989.

―――. *Space, Time and Medicine.* Boston: Shambala, 1982.

―――. "Prayer is Good Medicine." *The Saturday Evening Post,* Nov/Dec, 1997.

Eddington, Arthur. *Science and the Unseen World.* New York: Macmillan, 1929.

Eddy, Mary Baker. *Science and Health with Key to the Scriptures.* Boston: The Christian Science Publishing Society, 1971.

Eisler, Riane. *The Chalice and the Blade: Our History, Our Future.* San Francisco: Harper, 1987.

Ferris, Timothy. *The Mind's Sky.* New York: Bantam, 1992.

Feynman, Richard P. *QED: The Strange Theory of Light and Matter.* Princeton, NJ: Princeton University Press, 1988.

Freud, Sigmund. *Civilization and Its Discontents,* translated by James Strachey. New York: W. W. Norton, 1962.

————. *The Future of an Illusion,* translated by James Strachey. New York: W. W. Norton, 1962.

————. *Totem and Taboo,* translated by James Strachey. London: Routledge & Kegan Paul, 1961.

Gibson, Margaret. *Out in the Open.* Baton Rouge, LA: Louisiana State University Press, 1989.

Gleick, James. *Chaos Theory: Making a New Science.* New York: Viking, 1987.

Greene, Brian. *The Elegant Universe: Superstrings, Hidden Dimensions and the Quest for the Ultimate Theory.* New York: W. W. Norton, 1999.

Gribben, John. *Schrœdinger's Kittens and the Search for Reality: Solving the Quantum Mysteries.* New York: Little, Brown & Co., 1995.

Griffin, Susan. *The Eros of Everyday Life.* New York: Doubleday, 1995.

Guntrip, Harry. *Psychoanalytic Theory, Therapy and the Self: A Basic Guide to the Human Personality in Freud, Erikson, Klein, Sullivan, Fairbairn, Hartmann, Jacobson and Winnicott.* New York: Basic Books, 1973.

Harvey, Andrew. *Son of Man: The Mystical Path to Christ.* San Francisco: HarperSanFrancisco, 1999.

————, ed. *Teachings of the Christian Mystics.* Boston: Shambala, 1998.

Havel, Vaclav. *Living in Truth.* New York: Faber & Faber, 1986.

————. "Address at Independence Hall." *New York Times,* Op Ed Page, July 8, 1994.

Hawking, Stephen M. *A Brief History of Time.* New York: Bantam, 1988.

Heisenberg, Werner. *Physics and Philosophy.* New York: Harper Torchbooks, 1958.

Hockney, David. *Cameraworks.* New York: Alfred A. Knopf, 1984.

Hodges, Elizabeth J. *The Three Princes of Serendip*. New York: Atheneum, 1964.

Lynn Hoffman, *Foundation of Family Therapy*. New York: Basic Books, 1981.

———. "Constructing Realities." *Family Process*, 29(1), March 1990.

Horgan, John. "Can Science Explain Consciousness?" *Scientific American*, July 1994.

———. *The Undiscovered Mind: How the Human Brain Defies Replication, Medication and Explanation*. New York: Touchstone, 1999.

Hurston, Zora Neale. *Their Eyes Were Watching God*. New York: McGraw Hill, 2000.

Huxley, Aldous. *Doors of Perception*. New York: HarperCollins, 1990.

———. *The Perennial Philosophy*. New York: HarperCollins, 1990.

Jacobson, Neil S. "Contextualism is Dead: Long Live Contextualism." *Family Process*, Vol. 33, No. 1, March 1994.

Jauregui, Ann. "Nothing Needs Fixing," *IONS Noetic Sciences Review*, Sept/Nov 2002.

———. "Three Tales from Serendipity." *The Chrysalis Reader*, Fall 2002.

———. "The Dream of Matter." *Common Boundary*, Nov/Dec 1996.

Jaykar, Pupul. *Krishnamurti: A Biography*. San Francisco: Harper & Row, 1988.

Jeans, James. *The Mysterious Universe*. Cambridge, England: Cambridge University Press, 1931.

Jordan, Judith V., Alexandra G. Kaplan, Jean Baker Miller, Irene P. Stiver, and Janet L. Surrey. *Women's Growth in Connection*. New York: Guilford Press, 1991.

Kabat-Zinn, Jon. *Full Catastrophe Living: Using the Wisdom of Your Body and Mind to Face Stress, Pain and Illness*. New York: Delta, 1991.

Keller, Evelyn Fox. *A Feeling for the Organism: The Life and Work of Barbara McClintock*. New York: W. H. Freeman and Co., 1983.

Kernberg, Otto. *Borderline Conditions and Pathological Narcissism*. New York: Jason Aronson, Inc., 1975.

Kohut, Heinz. *The Restoration of the Self.* New York: International Universities Press, 1977.

Kothari, D. S. "Atom and the Self." *Proceedings of the Indian National Science Academy,* Part A, Physical Science 46:1, 1980.

Lawlor, Robert. *Voices of the First Day.* Rochester, VT: Inner Traditions, 1991.

Le Guin, Ursula. *Unlocking the Air and Other Stories.* New York: Harper-Collins, 1996.

Levy, Neil. *The Last Rebbe of Bialystok.* Berkeley, CA: Creative Arts Book Co., in publication.

Lukas, M. "The World According to Ilya Prigogine." *Quest/80,* December 1980.

Markides, Kyriacos C. *The Magus of Strovolos: The Extraordinary World of a Spiritual Healer.* New York: Penguin/Arkana, 1990.

Matousek, Mark. "The Teaching." *Common Boundary,* July/Aug 1995.

Mayer, Elizabeth Lloyd. "The Essential Subjectivity and Intersubjectivity of Clinical Facts." *International Journal of Psychoanalysis,* 77:4, 1996.

————. *Extraordinary Knowing: Making Sense of the Inexplicable in Everyday Life.* New York: Bantam Dell, in publication.

Miller, Jean Baker. *Toward a New Psychology of Women.* Boston: Beacon Press, 1987.

Mitchell, Edgar, and Dwight Williams (contributor). *The Way of the Explorer: An Apollo Astronaut's Journey Through the Material and Mystical Worlds.* New York: Putnam Publishing Group, 1996.

Napier, Augustus and Carl Whitaker. *The Family Crucible: The Intense Experience of Family Therapy.* New York: HarperCollins, 1988.

O'Hanlon, Bill. "The Third Wave: The Promise of Narrative." *Networker,* Nov/Dec 1994.

Oliver, Mary. *New and Selected Poems.* Boston: Beacon Press, 1992.

Olney, Dick. *Walking in Beauty,* Roslyn Moore, ed. Mendocino, CA: DO Publishing, 1996.

Penrose, Roger. *Shadows of the Mind: A Search for the Missing Science of Consciousness.* New York: Oxford University Press, 1994.

Phillips, Adam. *Terrors and Experts*. Cambridge, MA: Harvard University Press, 1996.

——. *On Kissing, Tickling and Being Bored: Psychoanalytic Essays on the Unexamined Life*. Cambridge, MA: Harvard University Press, 1993.

Pickering, George. *Creative Malady: Illness in the Lives and Minds of Charles Darwin, Florence Nightingale, Mary Baker Eddy, Sigmund Freud, Marcel Proust, and Elizabeth Barrett Browning*. New York: Delta, 1976.

Price, Reynolds. *A Whole New Life: An Illness and a Healing*. New York: Plume/Penguin, 1994.

——. *A Palpable God: Thirty Stories Translated from the Bible*. San Francisco: North Point Press, 1985.

Prigogine, Ilya and Isabelle Stengers. *Order Out of Chaos: Man's New Dialogue with Nature*. New York: Bantam Books, 1984.

Radin, Dean. *The Conscious Universe*. San Francisco: HarperSanFrancisco, 1997.

Ram Dass. *Be Here Now*. New York: Crown, 1971.

——, Mark Matousek, and Marlene Roeder. *Still Here: Embracing Aging, Changing and Dying*. New York: Riverhead, 1991.

Remen, Rachel Naomi. *My Grandfather's Blessings: Stories of Strength, Refuge and Belonging*. New York: Riverhead Books, 2000.

——. *Kitchen Table Wisdom: Stories That Heal*. New York: Riverhead Books, 1997.

Roszak, Theodore. *The Voice of the Earth*. New York: Simon & Schuster, 1992.

Schrœdinger, Erwin. *Mind and Matter*. Cambridge, England: Cambridge University Press, 1958.

Schwenk, Theodor. *Sensitive Chaos: The Creation of Flowing Forms in Water and Air*. London: Rudolf Steiner Press, 1999.

Scott-Maxwell, Florida. *The Measure of My Days*. New York: Penguin, 2000.

Sheldrake, Rupert. *The Presence of the Past: Morphic Resonance and the Habits of Nature*. Rochester, VT: Park Street Press, 1995.

————. *Seven Experiments That Could Change theWorld: A Do-It-Yourself Guide to Revolutionary Science.* New York: Riverhead Books, 1995.

————. "Awards for Research by Students." *Institute of Noetic Sciences Bulletin,* VI/3, Autumn 1991.

Sheldrake, Rupert, Terence McKenna, and Ralph Abraham. *The Evolutionary Mind: Trialogues at the Edge of the Unthinkable.* Santa Cruz, CA: Trialogue Press, 1998.

————. *Trialogues at the Edge of theWest: Chaos, Creativity and the Resacralization of theWorld.* Santa Cruz, CA: Trialogue Press, 1992.

Smith, Huston. *Why Religion Matters: The Fate of the Human Spirit in an Age of Disbelief.* San Francisco: HarperSanFrancisco, 2001.

————. *Cleansing the Doors of Perception: The Religious Significance of Entheogenic Plants and Chemicals.* New York: Jeremy P. Tarcher/Putnam, 2000.

————. *The World's Religions.* San Francisco: HarperSanFrancisco, 1991.

————. *Beyond the Post-Modern Mind.* Wheaton, IL: Quest Books, 1989.

————. *Forgotten Truth: The Primordial Tradition.* New York: Harper Colophon Books, 1976.

Stapp, Harry. "Bell's Theorem and World Process." *Il Nuovo Cimento,* 29B, 1975.

Stent, Gunther. *The Coming of the Golden Age: A View of the End of Progress.* Garden City, NY: The Natural History Press, 1969.

Talbot, Michael. *The Holographic Universe.* New York: HarperCollins, 1991.

Tarnas, Richard. *The Passion of the Western Mind: Understanding the Ideas That Have Shaped Our WorldView.* New York: Ballantine Books, 1991.

Trumbull, Richard. "Control Mastery and Self-Psychology: Will the Patient Please Stand Still." Presentation to San Diego Self Psychology Study Group, Spring 1993.

————. "When Talking Helps and When Talking Hurts: The Problem of Retraumatization in the Treatment of a Brother and Sister with Post Traumatic Stress Disorder." Presentation to San Diego Self Psychology Study Group, Spring, 1995.

Walters, Marianne et al. *The Invisible Web.* New York: Guilford Press, 1988.

Welty, Eudora. *The Wide Net and Other Stories.* New York: A Harvest Book, 1971.

Weiss, Joseph and Harold Sampson. *How Psychotherapy Works: Process and Technique.* New York: Guilford Press, 1993.

Weschler, Lawrence. *A Miracle, A Universe.* New York: Penguin Books, 1991.

White, Michael and David Epston. *Narrative Means to Therapeutic Ends.* New York: W. W. Norton, 1990.

Wilber, Ken, ed. *Quantum Questions: Mystical Writings of the World's Great Physicists.* Boston: Shambala, 1984.

Winnicott, D. W. *The Maturational Processes and the Facilitating Environment: Studies in the Theory of Emotional Development.* New York: International Universities Press, 1965.

————. *Through Pediatrics to Psychoanalysis.* New York: Basic Books, 1975.

Winterson, Jeanette. *Sexing the Cherry.* New York: Grove Press, 1998.

Woolf, Henry, ed. *The Analytic Spirit: Essays in the History of Science.* Ithaca, NY: Cornell University Press, 1990.

Wylie, Mary S. "Diagnosing for Dollars?" *Networker,* May/June 1995.

Zimmerman, Jeffrey L. and Victoria Dickerson. "Using a Narrative Metaphor: Implications for Theory and Clinical Practice." *Family Process,* September 1994.

Zucker, Ellen. "The Exaggerated Importance of Early Childhood Determinants of Adult Character Structure." Paper presented to Women's Therapy Center Symposium, "Feminists Critiquing Ourselves," Spring 1997.

INDEX

Abraham, Ralph, 141–
    142, 143, 152
Abstract, talking about, 4
Acupressure, 147–148
Alchemy, 67, 74
Alcott, Louisa May, 19
Aldebaran, 47–48, 51
Alternative therapies, 94
*Alternative Therapies in Health
    and Medicine,* 60
Ambiguity, 117, 118
American culture, Freud
    on, 85
American Psychiatric As-
    sociation, 95
Ammons, A. R., 123
Amyotrophic lateral scle-
    rosis (ALS),
    130–131
Angkor Wat, 156
Animals, powers of,
    182–183
Apollo spacecraft, 185,
    186
Aristotle, 142, 171–172
Art therapy, 95
"Atom and Self"
    (Kothari), 36–37
Atoms, 68

Attention, effects of, 163
Augustine, St., 180
Autonomous ego, 80

Baby, concept of, 106
Bateson, Gregory, 105
Bell, John Stewart, 27, 41
Benson, Herbert, 59–60,
    61–62
Berry, Wendell, 1
Bettelheim, Bruno, 83–84
Blake, William, 130
Blanck, Gertrude, 83
Blanck, Rubin, 83
Blue tits, story of,
    182–183
Body work, 95
Bohm, David, 170–171
Bohr, Neils, 126
Boundaries, 142
Boyle, Robert, 66
Brain, 78
Brandt, Bill, 99–100
Brandt, Noya, 99
Bruner, Edward, 110
"Butterfly Effect" theory,
    103
Byrd, Randolph,
    162–163

Cambodia, 144–147
    Leng, Sun, 153–155
    violence in, 155–156,
        157
Candidate stories, 115,
    118–119
Cartesian thinking,
    xii–xiii, 80
Central Valley, California,
    45
"Certain Philosophical
    Questions" (New-
    ton), 66, 67
Chaos
    Aristotle on, 142
    "Butterfly Effect" the-
        ory of, 103
    laws of chaos, 171
    need for, 142
    Newton on, 68,
        69–70, 142
Child abuse, 111
Chodron, Pema, 49
Chosen meanings, 115
Christian Science, 18–
    21. *See also* Eddy,
    Mary Baker
*Civilization and Its Discon-
    tents* (Freud), 85

Clairvoyance, 160
Clergy, stress and, 61
Clouds, generation of, 175–177
Cogito, 81–82
Collective unconscious, 64
Common Boundary conference, 96
Consciousness, 170–171
Constructing problems, 110
Control Mastery, 107–108
Copernicus, Nicolaus, 47–48
Creativity, 42–43
Curative action, 108
Curved space, 32
Cybernetics, 105

Dalai Lama, 177
Dark Ages, 40
Davidson, Dave, 13
Davies, Paul, 132
Death Valley, California, 45–49
Deconstructing problems, 110
Descartes, René, xii, 66, 80–83
Diagnostic and Statistical Manual of Mental Disorders (DSM-IV), 95–96
Dickinson, Emily, 19
Dillard, Annie, 33
Disabled people, 134–135
Discovery, tales of, 125–128
Disease
  Freud on, 86–87
  leprosy, 146–147
  prayer and, 164–165
  relaxation and, 60
Dissipative structures, 171
Distant intentionality, 162

Doors of Perception (Huxley), 159
Dossey, Larry, 34, 60, 162, 164–165
Dostoevsky, F., 86
Double awareness, 12
Dreams, 7

Earthquakes, 125
Eccles, J., 170
Eddington, Sir Arthur, 25
Eddy, Mary Baker, 19–20, 165
  Harris, Virginia on, 61
  Scientific Statement of Being, 21
Ego, 84
Einstein, Albert, 26, 27, 87, 125–126
  creativity and, 42
  scientific epiphany of, 128–129
Emerson, Ralph Waldo, 19, 36
Enlightenment, 62
The Enlightenment, 45
Epiphanies
  meaning of, 3–4
  occasioning, 159–160
  as prayer, 160, 173
Epston, David, 64
The Evolutionary Mind: Trialogues at the Edge of the Unthinkable (Sheldrake, McKenna & Abraham), 141
Existential psychotherapy, 95
Exposure therapy, 161

Fairies, 73–74
A Feeling for the Organism (Keller), 127
Ferris, Timothy, 11
Fibromyalgia, 93
Flatow, Ira, 26
Forgetting what helps, 61–62

Foucault, Michel, 110
Fractals, 140–142, 152
Freud, Anna, 84
Freud, Sigmund, 44, 63–64, 83–87
  Bettelheim, Bruno on, 83–84
  mind, looking for, 83
  religion, questions of, 181
  soul, notion of, 83, 117
  translations of, 84
Freud and Man's Soul (Bettelheim), 83–84
Frost, Robert, 140

Galileo, 49–50
Gibson, Margaret, 17
Glass, Leon, 170–171
Glove anesthesia, 85
God. *See* Religion
Golden Canyon, 46–49
Gould, Steven Jay, xiii
Grace Cathedral, San Francisco, 163–164
Grace-filled moments, 181
Gravity, 67
Greenberger, Daniel, 26, 33
Gribben, John, 26
Griffin, Susan, 63
Grown-up, concept of, 106

Hadler, Norman, 91–94
Hale-Bopp Comet, 45, 46, 51
Hallmarks of human maturity, 110
Hand reading, 79–80
Hard sciences, 63
Harris, Virginia, 60–61
Harvard Medical School, 59
Havel, Vaclav, 101, 102
Hawking, Stephen, 42, 130–131
  talk by, 133–135

Healing Words: the Power of Prayer and the Practice of Medicine (Dossey), 162
Heisenberg, Werner, 126–127, 141
Hermetic tradition, 67, 68
Herodotus, 3
Hockney, David, 99–100, 103
Human attention, 163
Human potential movement, 95
Hun Sen, 157
Hurston, Zora Neale, xi
Huxley, Aldous, 151, 159

Identity, 152
Illness. *See* Disease
Indian National Science Academy, 36
Infinity, 119–120
    fractals and, 142
Information theory, 105
Innate spirit, 139
The Inquisition, 49–50
Institute of Noetic Sciences, 60, 185
Interpretive knowledge, 115
Intuition, 160
Inuit people, 180
Irritable bowel syndrome, 93

James, Henry, 19
James, William, 19
Jeans, Sir James, 53
Jin Shin Jiutsu, 180
John Paul II, Pope, 50
Joy and sorrow, 37–38
Jung, Karl, 64

Kabat-Zinn, Jon, 72
Keller, Evelyn Fox, 127
Kernberg, Otto, 106

Knowing
    again, knowing, 184
    gift for, 157–158
Kohut, Heinz, 107
Kosslyn, Stephen, 61
Kothari, D. S., 36–37
Krishnamurti, 172

Lakota people, 12–13
Laws of chaos, 171
Lederberg, Joshua, 129
LeGuin, Ursula, 39
Leng, Sun, 153–155
Leprosy, 146–147
Levy, Neil, 52
Liquid time, 32
Long-distance prayer, 60
Lorenz, Edward, 103

McClintock, Barbara, 127–128, 129
McKenna, Terence, 137, 141
Magic, 67
Massage in Cambodia, 146–147
Mathematics, 132–133
Matter
    mind-matter-time, 32
    as phenomenon of thought, 61
Mayer, Elizabeth, 108
Mechthilde of Magdeburg, 159
Meditation, 72
Mental Research Institute of Palo Alto, 105
Metaphors, 41
Mexico, Festival of the Virgin, 180–181
Microscopic world, 29–30
Microtubules, 43
Mikhalkov, Nikita, 117
Milky Way, 141
Miller, Jean Baker, 106
Mind, 78–80
    abnormalities of, 90–91

Mind-body experimentation, 62
The Mind/Body Medical Institute, 59
Mind-matter-time, 32
Miracles, 180
Mitchell, Edgar, 185–186
Morphic fields, 183
Music, talking about, 4, 6
The Mysterious Universe (Jeans), 53
Mystical writings, 41–42

Narrative therapy, 108
Nature, powers of, 36
Newton, Isaac, 50–51, 65–70, 171–172
    on chaos, 142
    mental breakdown of, 66–67
    poetry of, 75
    as revelator, 69–70
Nin, Anaïs, 118
Nondiaphanous edges, 141
Nondirected prayer, 34–35, 160
Nonlocality theorem, 27, 28
Non sequiturs, 8–9
Northern California Association of Family Therapists, 108
Northridge Earthquake, 125

Objective reality, 64, 109
Observer/observed relationship, 26–27, 32
Oliver, Mary, 104
Olney, Dick, 148–152, 165–166
One Mind, 36–37
Opticks (Newton), 66
Orpingalik, 8

Pain, imagery and, 61
Pathogenic beliefs, 107–108

Penrose, Roger, 42–43, 132–133
The Perennial Philosophy (Huxley), 151
Perennial therapy, 151–152
Person, concept of, 106–107
Personality, 152
Personal truth, xiii–xiv
PET scans, 78
Phillips, Adam, 77, 115–117, 118, 143
Phnom Penh, 144–147
Physics and Philosophy (Heisenberg), 141
Picasso, Pablo, 43–44
Plato, 67
Pol Pot, 153
Pond water, 29–30
Popper, Karl, 170
Postmodernism
concept of, 103–104
defined, 101–102
world views and, 118
Post-traumatic stress disorder (PTSD), 161–162
Prayer
clerical stress and, 61
disease and, 164–165
efficacy of, 160
epiphanies and, 160, 173
illness and, 164–165
long-distance prayer, 60
post-traumatic stress disorder (PTSD) and, 161–162
San Francisco General Hospital study, 162–163
Prayer life, 34–35
Price, Reynolds, 7, 8
Prigogine, Ilya, 171
Principia (Newton), 69
Protest, history of, 111

Psyche, 85
Psychedelic experimentation, 95
Psychoanalysis, 52
"Psychoanalysis and the Future of Fear" (Phillips), 115–116
Psychotherapy
camps of theorists, 104–105
chaos theory and, 143
definition of, 90
functions of, 107
postmodern psychotherapy, 118–119
Psychotropic drugs, 161
Ptolemy, 48
Purpose, sense of, 139–140
Pythagoreans, 67

Quantum mechanics, 25–26, 40–41, 142
Bohm, David on, 171–172
Quantum Questions (Wilber), 41–42
Queries (Newton), 69
Quimby, Phineas Parkhurst, 19
hands, healing with, 86

Ram Dass, 90, 96–97
Reading minds, 79
Reality, 39–40
objective reality, 64, 109
science and, 42, 44
Reed College, 62
Relativity, 142
Bohm, David on, 171–172
Relaxation, disease and, 60
Religion
Freud, questions of, 181

Hawking, Stephen on, 134
Newton, Isaac on, 68–69
Religious healing, 95
Resonance in room, 163–164
Revelation stories, 39–40

Sampson, Harold, 107–108
San Francisco General Hospital, 162–163
Sathi, Spyros, 180
Satir, Virginia, 105
Schizophrenia, 105
Schlitz, Marilyn, 60
Schroedinger, Erwin, 43
Science
modern science, 102
reality and, 40
soft sciences, 63
Scientific Age, 50
Scientific Statement of Being, 21
Scott-Maxwell, Florida, 175
Secularism, 132
Self
awareness of, 12–13
Kernberg, Otto on, 106
sense of, 80
Self-acceptance, 149, 152
Self-Acceptance training, 149
Self-image, 152
distortions posed by, 153
Self Psychology, 107
Sellars, Peter, 125
Sense of self, 80
Separation-individuation, 80
Serendipity, 182
Shamanic healing, 95
Shapeshift, 26
Sheldrake, Rupert, 141, 182–184

Sierra Nevada Mountains, 45
Silent prayer, 162
Silver Bay, 11–24
Smith, Huston, 115, 156–158
Smith, Kendra, 156
Soft sciences, 63
Sorrow and joy, 37–38
Soul
    Descartes on, 80–81
    Freud on, 83, 117
Spirituality. *See also* Prayer; Religion
    disease and, 60
    "Spirituality and Healing in Medicine" conference, 59
Spitzer, Robert, 96
The Standard Edition of the Complete Psychological Works of Sigmund Freud, 84
Stereograms, 123–124
Stevens, Norman, 100
Stories, 7
    collage of stories, person's life as, 118–119
    fairies, 74

about ourselves, 54–56
post-traumatic stress disorder (PTSD) and, 161–162
sets of, 114
Strachey, James, 84
Superego, 84
Surprise, moments of, 186
Sydenham, Thomas, 92, 94
Synchronicities, 64
Systems theory, 95

Talbot, Michael, 131
Tamasese, Kiwi, 99
Telepathy, 160
Telescope, 49
Thoreau, Henry David, 19
"The Three Princes of Serendip," 182
Tibetan Buddhists, 12–13
Time travel, 134
Tradition, science and, 44
Transcendent experience, 36
    quantum imagery and, 43
Trembling moment, 8
Truth, xiii

Twain, Mark, 94
Twelfth Night, 3

Unconscious
    notion of, 85–86
    Quimby, Phineas Parkhurst on, 86
Unconscious prayer, 162
Uniqueness of individual, 80

Visual imagery, 61

Walpole, Horace, 182
Weiss, Joseph, 107–108
Welty, Eudora, 59
Whiston, William, 68
Whitaker, Carl, 106–107
Whitaker, Muriel, 107
White, Michael, 64, 108, 109–111
    on hierarchy, 118
Why Religion Matters (Smith), 156
Wilber, Ken, 41–42
Winnicott, Donald, 106
Winterson, Jeanette, 87
The World's Religions (Smith), 156

ABOUT THE

AUTHOR

Ann Jauregui, Ph.D., has been a practicing psychotherapist, consultant, and teacher in Berkeley, California, for the past twenty years.

An early sketch of her book, an essay entitled "The Dream of Matter," won the Common Boundary Research Award "for making an outstanding contribution to the integration of psychology and spirituality." Her essays have appeared in *Common Boundary*, *Dulwich Centre Newsletter*, *Institute of Noetic Sciences Review* and *The Chrysalis Reader*.

She and her husband, John, a primary care physician who shares her interest in an inclusive approach to wellness, boast eight married children and twelve grandchildren. The family spends quiet time and not-so-quiet time in northern New Mexico and the Sierra.